GOD'S LAWS DON'T HAVE LOOPHOLES

GOD'S LAWS DON'T HAVE LOOPHOLES

That's Why We Sing Amazing Grace

David H. Benke

CPH®

SAINT LOUIS

Library of Congress Cataloging-in-Publication Data

Benke, David H., 1946
    God's laws don't have loopholes / David H. Benke.
      p. cm.
    ISBN 0-570-04578-9
    1. Perfection—Religious aspects—Christianity. 2. God—Love.
  3. Spiritual life—Christianity.   I. Title
BT766.B46   1995
    234—dc20
                               94-28515

1 2 3 4 5 6 7 8 9 10   04 03 02 01 00 99 98 97 96 95

To my mom

**Dorothea Wilhelmine Beata Boerger
Benke**

Uniquely Alive in Christ

Contents

GOD'S LAWS DON'T HAVE LOOPHOLES

 **Chapter 1**

The Search for Perfection

Be ye therefore perfect, even as your
Father which is in heaven is perfect.
Matthew 5:48 KJV

To be perfect means that you are the absolute best. No flaws. No errors. No glitches. No negatives. When I consider my personal quest for perfection, it's enough to make me laugh ... or cry ... or both. Yet God *demands* perfection from all of us. To discover God's design for human life, the search for perfection must be undertaken.

"You've got to help me! I mean it! It wasn't my fault—I was driving *perfect!*"

The midnight caller just about blew my ear off. Benke's phone rule: If it's after 11:00 p.m. it's either a West Coast relative or a major problem. I surmised that this was going to be a problem.

"What are you talking about?" I soothed into the phone. "Tell me about it."

"It's me, Steve," the caller replied. "I'm driving cab now. Quit the pizza thing; not enough ready cash. And I'm out on the expressway, doing the speed limit—*no more*—I'm not kidding; just driving *perfect*. And this guy on a motorcycle with his girlfriend ... Whoosh! They fly right past me! Then the guy in the car in front of me, a brown Taurus, I think ... Pow! He hits the brakes!...And bang! They take off right through his rear window. I mean, right through it. I'm telling you, Rev., it wasn't my fault! I was driving *perfect*.

"But I know they're hurt bad. Could you find out who they are and maybe visit them? And then maybe let me know how they're doing?"

"Hey, Steve," I interrupt, "sounds like you're really shook up. I'll tell you this much. I'll do what ... "

"Yeah, please, do what you can, okay? Because really, it wasn't my fault. I was driving *perfect*," Steve wails that word one last time.

Human Perfection?

Perfect. The absolute best. No flaws, no errors, no negatives, no glitches. Can you relate to the tightness in my midnight caller's throat? I know I can. We all feel threatened when confronted with perfection. We've all got our learner's permits, motoring down the interstates and off-ramps of life. And, if the truth is told, much of our motoring is far from perfect. We weave. We wobble. We sputter, "Accidents will happen." We are out there causing our share of accidents, from fender benders to major bangers to fatalities—even our own. We know we are far from perfect. We know down deep we are fatally flawed, and it bothers us. Considering the concept of perfection causes a twinge, a shudder, down someplace deep in our soul.

I know that when I ponder perfection and me, I've either got to laugh or cry … or both. Perfection just hasn't happened. Not that I haven't tried. It's just that I cannot handle it. As the apostle Paul put it, "What I do is not the good I want to do; no, the evil I do not want to do—this I keep on doing" (Romans 8:19). I argue when I should keep my mouth shut. I cut people off because I just can't wait to tell them how to solve their problems *my* way. I keep making the same mistakes over and over again.

It Can Be Embarrassing

Sometimes imperfection is almost laughable. Notice that I said "almost." Embarrassing probably better describes it, and embarrassing moments are best laughed at in long hindsight.

Embarrassing imperfection is magnified if you do your thing in the public eye. My congregation here in Brooklyn worships in two languages on a weekly basis, English and Spanish. Being raised in Milwaukee, Wisconsin, by parents of German descent made it nigh unto impossible for me to have Spanish as a native tongue. But I have tried. I speak a passable Spanish, but still call my Spanish/English dictionary a very close friend.

Recently I was preaching my Spanish-language Palm Sunday sermon. The church was full and buzzing with excitement. Sixteen youngsters in suits and white dresses sat in the front rows, prepared to come forward for Holy Communion for the first time.

All their loved ones were seated just behind them, so I wanted to get things just right ... you know, *perfect*. Into the wee hours of the morning, I had translated exact phrases from English into Spanish.

I began the sermon with these words: "Este es un día festivo, un día *de mojón*." And the place erupted ... not in applause, but in laughter. Men stood up, waving their arms, shouting through their chuckles, "No, no!" Women shrieked. The kids went out of control, laughing and screaming. The congregational elder, seated over on the other side of the altar, kind of hopped across the sanctuary attempting to stop the sermon. This suited me just fine, as I watched the good citizens of the Kingdom falling down in the aisles over my introductory words.

"What in the world?" I thought to myself, mystified. All I had said was, "This is a festival day—a milestone day." Perfect beginning for a Palm Sunday sermon, no? Not quite. It turns out that there is an alternative meaning to the word *milestone,* or *mojón,* a meaning not readily encountered in the dictionary. It is a more popular meaning, however. *Mojón,* you see, is the common household word for doggy doo!

This is not exactly the perfect thing to say to girls in white dresses on a dewy Palm Sunday morning. I suppose I could have checked it out in advance, but I thought, "Why bother? It's right there in the dictionary." I will not soon forget that experience. It ranks right up there among my most embarrassing, most humiliating moments in public speaking. And I thought I had it right, perfectly right!

Victims of Imperfect Circumstances

Not only are *we* far from perfect, a point I believe I have just proven in "milestone" manner, we live in a *world* full of problems, failures, and glitches. Life is just not perfect, is it? Like Steve, the midnight cabbie, there are times, and many of them, when through no fault of our own bad things happen, even tragic events.

During a recent week in our church's day-care center all of the following went on the blink: the refrigerator, the computer, the copier, the tele-phones, the sewer, and the toilets. Oh, yes, lest I forget, someone walked off with the typewriters as well. It was one of those weeks when all conver-sations were halted in mid-sentence:

"I guess I'll call … No, can't call. No phones."

"Let me type up … Whoops! Okay, who hid the typewriter?"

"Make 20 copies … Hmm, better yet, why don't you just hand-write the original 20 times."

"Bring it up on the compu … Oh, forget it!"

"Just a second. I need a break. I've got to go … home!"

By the end of the week the entire staff was so frustrated we voted on buying a cabin in the mountains and forever leaving society with its plugs and bugs.

Only the repairmen took joy in the imperfections of our machines. Our complete frustration was, after all, their meal ticket. Many are the blessed, from doctors and lawyers to plumbers and auto mechanics, who flourish from life's imperfections.

No, if you are seeking perfection, much more often than not, you are going to find the following replacement package: embarrassment, frustration, or, at the deepest level, despair. Fear and trembling, disillusionment and despair make their appearance when the perfect marriage dissolves in a bulletlike hail of accusations, the perfect child drops out of school, the perfect job is terminated. Like a cabdriver on the interstate who is there when the motorcycle veers out of control, you can become paralyzed by an imperfectly awful situation. And then the cry goes up: "God. Oh, God! Why? Why *me?* It's not supposed to be this way!"

We cry in the dark because we know that there are standards. And at some level we are aware, if only dimly, that we're not up to them, and that the whole blooming globe is rolling like a lunatic out of control on a course of self-destruction. How do we respond? How can we handle it? How can we cope with these standards, with regulations and boundaries we must exceed and cannot seem to heed?

Defense Mechanisms

If we live each day striving after the goal of perfection, we will most certainly not be "happy campers." It has been said that our mental hospitals are filled primarily with guilty people who have not been able to measure up to the perfection trip that someone laid on them. So we have to find mechanisms to cope. We have to discover some way of getting out from under. Here's a list of three or four of our common attempts to cope:

1. Keep busy and don't think about it. Follow the advice of the renowned poet and philosopher Alfred E. Neuman, who said, "What, me worry?"

Unfortunately, I am here to tell you that the wolf is at the door. You have cause for concern. You are permitted to worry.

2. Laugh it off. Reason it out, "Hey, who's perfect anyway? Only Bo Derek was a perfect 10, and I'll bet by now she's only an 8.5." Such laughter, though, becomes nervous in a hurry. Facts are not faced.

3. When facts are not faced, escape plans are

hatched. Where I live in inner-city Brooklyn, imperfection would be a major jump *up* from what most folks face every day. It's a horror show. Many, hemmed in and hassled on all sides, fall victim to self-induced plans to escape the pain and the anger. These false plans hatch nightmares. Some stick a needle in their veins. Some stick a gun in your face. Some seek relief in the bottom of a bottle. The false escape hatch is but a door to violent despair.

4. In the teeth of all this, it is most tempting to simply lower your expectations. "Well," you drop your aim as you raise your voice, "who's perfect? *Nobody,* that's who. So as long as you're good and trying hard, that's enough. That will have to be enough. And it puts me miles ahead of most people anyway. So there!"

This is the most normal human response to encounters with the concept of perfection. And, like so much of our thinking, it is both *perfectly right* and yet *totally wrong.* What is perfectly *right* is that there is nobody who is perfect. What is *totally wrong* is believing that being good and trying hard is enough.

God's Demand for Perfection

God will not permit us the easy out. There are standards, and we do not get to set them. These standards have been set for us. They are just. They are, in fact, perfect. And they are final. It is Jesus, the self-proclaimed "Truth," who finally stops all traffic. "Be ye therefore perfect," he commands, "even as your Father which is in heaven is perfect" (Matthew 5:48 KJV).

Notice what Jesus *doesn't* say. He doesn't say,

"Be ye good."
"Be ye okay."
"Be ye number two and try harder."
"Be ye in the top 10 percent."
"Be ye better than the guy next door or the bum in the gutter."

No. "Be ye therefore *perfect,*" says the Lord. Therefore any encounter with perfection leads to a confrontation with the living God. Let me repeat that in bold letters: **Any encounter with perfection leads to a confrontation with the living God.** That is the bottom line. Such an encounter is *demanded* by the very same God.

In addition, the statement "Be ye therefore perfect" is not a finished statement. There is more to it. It is not a command without consequences. I am sure you can fill in the rest. The full statement is, "Be ye therefore perfect … or else!"

At face value this is not comforting news, is it? I put it in different terms one Sunday in a sermon: "Do you have to be perfect," I asked, "to get to heaven?"

Now Lutherans, as a block of 10 million or so in the United States, normally do not have dialog between pulpit and pew. Our congregation is a little bit different, though, so we do talk to one another during sermons. This time there was a strong outburst.

"No!" was the unanimous reply. Little kids who sass their moms shook their heads, "No way!"

Recovering addicts, who turn lights out on perfection and goodness when they jam substance-filled needles into their arms, realistically proclaimed, "No chance."

Senior citizens who have experienced poor health, loss of friends, and the ensuing bitterness and emptiness shook their heads firmly. "No indeed."

Upstanding citizens who just finished confessing "Cleanse thou me from secret faults" as they remembered 30 or 40 unclean corners of the soul thought, "No, it won't work."

Like a good preacher, I waited until they were finished nodding, shaking, and retorting. Then I paused for effect.

"Do you have to be perfect," I repeated, "to get to heaven? The answer is simple. Yes, you do!"

People jumped back. Their mouths flew open. They gazed in astonishment. "Whoa! Hold up, Preach. What are you talking about? You know us, sitting out here, and you know we're not perfect. And, let's tell it true, neither are you! So who are you kidding? If we have to be perfect, how can we get to heaven? If we have to be perfect, how can we be right with God?"

These are precisely the questions we are going to tackle together. We will have to face our deepest fears straight ahead. Are you with me?

Digging Deep for Lasting Treasure

Yes, when you ponder perfection, there is a troubling of the waters. Probably right about now your mind has begun to run through a little checklist of your own imperfections. The human mind is funny that way—diving into the stream of personal memories muddying the waters, bringing you up gasping for air. Bringing you up with stuff from the bottom of the pond. Who wants to remember those things? Yet they wash over you like a rushing stream carrying you off, don't they?

The examination of perfection will definitely take you out of your comfort zone. Now I have to tell you that not only will it get worse, but there also is no way around it. We must get to the bottom of this confrontation between you and the living God. We must dig deep. It will be, at first, painful. Nevertheless, for the sake of your destiny, it must be done. Later, down the line, our search will result in a simply amazing discovery. At the most profound depths there is a priceless treasure. His name is Jesus.

Directions for the Search

To engage in a thorough search for perfection before the living God—that is our task. I propose we begin by looking at the way things are as they naturally occur. How does the human heart deal with the demands of all the standards it runs up against? What echoes does that tiny boom box called your conscience ring up? Where does reason lead you in your search for perfection?

Then we must look to the written standard called the Law of God. This is his nonnegotiable deal with each and every one of us, contained in a book called the Bible. How do we stand up against that code book?

Then I must usher you into court. Oh, yes, there is a courtroom scene in your search for perfection. If God sets standards, then there must be penalties for failing to live up to them, not so? Count on this—the courtroom scene is *the* central event in your life. The living God will be revealed in full in that courtroom. From there we will proceed to the judge's chambers to discuss your verdict. Finally, back outside the chambers, we will begin to walk the perfect life. Are you ready? Let's go!

When I keep calling on you to meet "the living God," I make the assumption that you believe in a "God" outside yourself. In other words, I assume that you acknowledge the existence of a higher power. If my assumption is mistaken, I would like to invite you to continue to read on anyway. This is going to be a "sugar-free" meeting with the one you do not as yet know or trust. You will be stretched well beyond the reality boundaries set by the mental gymnastics and inner aerobics of this "feel-good generation." You will see things as they really are.

If, on the other hand, you are a believer, I urge you to stay tightly tuned as well. Check the fundamentals of your faith against what will be told you now. Check hard. Dig in. Walk on.

 **Chapter 2**

Why Is Everybody Always Picking on Me?

The man said, "The woman you put here with me—she gave me some fruit from the tree, and I ate it." Genesis 3:12

By nature we wiggle, especially when it comes to facing up to our responsibilities before God. We wiggle because the seat upon which we perch is hot. God is God, and we are not. And it makes us squirm.

Once upon the planet earth there was perfection. It was absolutely awe-inspiring. The birds chirped in orchestrated harmony. It only rained at night. There was no rush-hour traffic. In fact, no one was rushing. Every room was a room with a view, because there was no end to the rooms available. Pollutants in the air? Perish the thought! The fossils from which fossil fuels derive were not yet a gleam in daddy dinosaur's eyes. The system was perfect. The world was perfect. It was so perfect that the Lord God, who created it all from scratch, in the cool of the day took regular constitutional walks through this garden environment.

The most exemplary aspect of the universal perfection back then at the beginning was the relationship between God and humankind. Of course, there were just two representatives of humankind at the time. Their names, as you may well know, were Adam and Eve. Everyone was on a first-name basis. Everything was out in the open. There were no secrets. There were no hostilities. Just as the lion did not look at the lamb and envision lamb chops, so Adam and Eve and the Lord God strolled together in the garden and conversed without carving one another up.

Passing the Buck

However, there were standards. Adam had been told he could eat fruit from any tree in the garden; but that he must not eat from the tree of the knowledge of good and evil or he would surely die. This was a standard commandment, of the type that says, "Do this; don't do this ... or else." In fact, it is not even a difficult commandment on the surface. Only one tree was off-limits. No doubt, Adam told Eve too what God had said.

Of course, you know the story. It took only *one* temptation to produce a fall. It took only *one* bite from forbidden fruit to pierce paradise with pain.

This is the story of the end of human perfection. It is the story of the long tumble, of the beginning of the end that we call death. It is the story of the radical rupture in the relationship between humankind and God. That rupture is called sin. It is the true story carried in our bones, in our genetic structure, in our spirits and in our thoughts, words, and deeds until this very day.

What we carry in our bones is an inherent tendency to wiggle, courtesy of the three characters in the opening act—Adam, Eve, and the serpent. Consider what happened. The commandment was made. The commandment was broken. And immediately, the instinct for survival led to secrecy, lying, and buck-passing by the lawbreakers.

It's almost comical. Imagine two kids and their pet dog, Scruffy, lined up at Dad's command against the kitchen wall next to the open cookie jar. Three chins are covered with chocolate. Yet when Dad inquires, "All right, now—who's responsible for this?" two fingers point like pistons at Scruffy. The doggy made them do it!

So the Lord God hands the baton to Adam, to whom the commandment was given. "Have you eaten from the tree that I commanded you not to eat from?" And Adam cannot bring himself simply to own up. He passes that baton. He flings that hot potato, trying like crazy to re-direct the heat-seeking missile of God's truth. "The woman," he responds. "The woman *you* put here with me—she gave me some fruit from the tree." Adam passes the baton down to his dearly beloved spouse, bone of his bones and rib from his ribs, and he directs that baton back *up* to the Boss. This is certainly the doubly bad idea of a desperate man.

And the woman, Eve? She cannot contain herself. "The serpent deceived me." Scruffy did it. Pass that baton on down the line.

Of course, all the snake could do was wiggle. It is this characteristic that seems to have been passed right on up the line to Eve and Adam. And to you. And to me. The demands of God reveal our imperfections, which will not go away. Owning up, instead, gives way to wiggling.

I see this wiggling in myself and others all the time.

Recently I called two members of our church youth group into my office for a little conversational conduct check. These two are simply unable to get along with each other. Meetings are interrupted, words are tossed like knives, lines are drawn on the concrete, sides are taken, everybody suffers. You know the story.

So I begin, "Well, what have you two got to say for yourselves?"

No response. Four eyes peering at shoelaces. Repeat the question. No response. Same eyes. Same shoelaces.

"Look at me, please!" I implore. Four eyes slowly meet mine, then quickly glance off at the wall, at the desk, through the window, anywhere else.

Finally Linda speaks. "That's a nice plaque you've got there on the wall. I didn't know you were a doctor. Wow!"

Nancy chimes in, "Could I call my sister? It'll only take a minute."

"Don't change the subject!" I explode. "What's with you two? We're here to talk about your fighting. Forget the plaque. Forget the phone."

"What I don't get," Nancy counters, "is why you're always picking on us two. Like we're the only ones who don't get along."

"Yeah, she's right!" Linda joins the newly formed club.

"Whoa, now!" I reply. "Think you're going to gang up on me? This is not about me or anybody else. It's just about you two."

After a pause, Linda chips in, biting off each word, "It's her fault—period. I'm just minding my own business, and she starts with me." She glares at Nancy.

Nancy retorts, "Minding your business! I wish for once you *would* mind your business instead of mine. You're the one!"

And they're off—wiggling, squirming, passing the baton, picking and poking, doing everything possible to avoid admitting the blame, to avoid confronting the truth about their behavior.

Not only are Linda and Nancy typical teenagers, they are typical human beings. We are by nature, through Adam and Eve, wigglers. In the heat of the moment, in the jumble and tangle of the imperfections closing around us, we constantly attempt to squirm free, to escape blame. Particularly when it comes to facing up to our responsibilities to perfection before God, we wiggle. God is God, and we are not, and it makes us squirm.

God, Why Are You Picking on Me?

In the quiet moments late at night, I often find myself squirming when considering the imperfections of the day and my all-too-impressive role in them. After running up and down and back and forth through the mental gymnastics of my escape-the-blame routine, I end up on the floor in a one-on-one wrestling match, an internal debate with God. I always end up facing off with God because my perception is that God is the source of all these imperfect moments. He's behind it. He's picking on me.

My internal debate is structured something like this:

Me: Okay, God, I admit it: I'm not perfect. But then, neither is anybody else. So what are you going to do, fry us all? I mean, there have to be some gradations, some levels, some steps on the ladder. Do you know what I mean? After all, I am an ordained clergyman. That ought to put me at least on the third or fourth rung, right?

God: Wrong rung. You're not even on the ladder, my son. It is true, "All have sinned and fall short of the glory of God." I am that God.

And "There is no one who does good, not even one." No one—not even you. The result is very simple. "The soul who sins is the one who will die." Period. And, I might add, so far the percentages read: Souls that have sinned—100 percent; deaths—100 percent.

Me: All right, all right. I catch your drift. Then let me put it to you this way: What can I do to make it up to you? Let me *do* something. Allow me to *donate,* from my own sparse personal accounts, a significant thank offering. Let me pay you off—er—up. Make amends. Anything. You name it.

God: You do not possess that much money. I am well aware of the sparseness of your bank account. There is not, however, that much money in all the banks of Switzerland. There are not that many reserves beneath the oil-rich sands of the Arabian desert. At any rate, "All [your] righteous acts are like filthy rags." Remember, "The soul who sins is the one who will die." Does that not pertain to you?

Me: That Bible passage has been used already. Let's not beat it to death. Now I'm getting the message; but I must say, I don't really agree with it at all. This is just not fair. And you are, above all else, fair. Right? Let me tell you what's not fair. *You* created me. Therefore *you* know my inherent weaknesses. *You* put me in the middle of all these impossible situations. I do my level best, but occasionally—I repeat, occasionally—I mess up. But *you* put me there.

And *you* are the one who gave me all these "Thou shalts" and "Thou shalt nots." You know I can't keep them. You know I can't be perfect. You hold me accountable. It's a setup. It's just not fair. I demand a fair hearing! Who are *you* to judge me? All the bad guys in the world, and you pick on me. Why are you picking on *me?*

(*There is absolute, deafening silence from God; see chapter 7.*)

Not listening, huh? Then I opt out. I won't play. I don't even believe you're there. It's a lousy game, and it's been set up so that religious types get to wag their fingers at normal people making the normal human mistakes, and then they take our guilt money to build bigger and better parking lots next to their cathedrals. I'm on to this, even though I'm part of it. Which only makes me madder, by the way. And I am plenty mad, believe me!

God: Do yourself a favor. Never underestimate me.

End of internal one-on-one conversation.

The Texas Side Step

Ever seen a big man who can dance well? We're all used to the Fred Astaires and the Gene Kellys, slim and athletic. But when a big fella cuts the rug in that dapper way only a dancer can, it's special. Charles Durning, the actor, is one such artist. Playing a glide-and-wink politician in a forgettable movie, he dances a number called the Texas Side Step. Up and down the courthouse steps he slides and pokes and shimmies and shakes. Give a little here, take it back there; he's telling us that the good life has to do with knowing how to keep your feet moving so as not to get stuck in the deep stuff.

Well, podnuhs, when it comes to meeting up with the living God, we're all side steppers. I have those quick feet, that soft shoe, and so do you. There's a little of that twinkle-toed Texas politician in all of us. We're not really anxious for a shoot-out encounter with the Almighty, so we dance the shuffle, then dash for cover. Do you want examples?

The conversation can go this way: "God? Oh, I don't think God's got much time for me, friend. Not with the situation in the Middle East and all. Look at Africa—millions of people and nothing to eat. And the inner cities right here in the USA. God's a little too busy for me. Hey, I've gotta run myself—maybe we'll talk some other time."

Religion is a surefire conversation killer. Why is that? Because people get nervous—and not just because they don't want to listen to someone else's convictions. No, they are just nervous. Why? Because if you start thinking too much about God, where is it going to get you? Into a deep hole, that's where. Into a spot where quick feet will only churn you down deeper. Better to dart quickly to other, safer topics.

Let's consider another turn of the conversation: "*Perfect.* You're telling me that God wants me to be perfect. I'll have to think about that. Tell you what, though: I'm good. Is 'good' good enough? Because I am good. I've given to the Community Chest, I'm in the VFW; I cut my lawn every Saturday, rain or shine; I fly the flag proudly; I love my wife. I'm good. Let me put it a better way: I've been blessed. I have my health and my family, drive a nice car, make a decent paycheck. Apparently God is behind me, backing me up all the way. That's good enough."

Mom, apple pie, the flag, and Chevrolet. We're all patriots when it comes to goodness. No one can deny the quest for goodness. Better good than bad, right? But notice how we've waltzed away from "Be ye therefore *perfect.*" We bunny-hopped over to the sunny side of the street, where the good guys ease on down the road.

The question is, is good sufficient? If it has to do with your golf swing, your voting record, your ability to hunt for bargains, your agility with numbers on the job, or the incredible way you can juggle that 9–5 job with raising three kids on a semi-starvation salary, the answer is yes. You *are* good.

However, if it has to do with standing before God and making a case for the goodness you need to gain a satisfactory relationship with the Almighty, then the answer is a thumping **no.** Good will not do.

Pulling the Wool

When will we be done dancing the side step? When will we wind down the wiggling? The answer is simple: Never. The philosopher Blaise Pascal said, "When we turn away from external nature and contemplate man inwardly, what then do we find? A creature riddled with contradiction, uncertainty, folly, and misery. Man wants to be great, and sees himself small. *He wants to be perfect, and he sees himself full of imperfections.*" This profound *dis*comfort with honest internal reflection leads to an interesting phenomenon. We try to pull the wool over our own eyes! It's bad enough trying to pull the wool over someone else's eyes, to prevent others from seeing something we don't want them to see. But we end up blindfolding *ourselves,* so great is the fear of seeing what is inside. Of course, you can still see inside. It's just that you don't want to.

Let me illustrate. A guy from the neighborhood came up to me one morning to ask me for money.

"Please, Rev, I need $30." So began the waltz.

"When do you need it?" I curtsied.

"Now, today, *right* now." He bowed.

"What's the problem?" I parried.

"Oh, the usual, you know." He twirled.

"I've got to know exactly what the problem is." I swooped.

"You know me—it's everything." He swirled.

"Tell me *one* thing." I swept on down the floor. Finally, after about 10 minutes of us shimmying around, he broke.

"Rev, you know why I want the money. I need a hit. I need a fix. I've got to score me some drugs."

The dance was over. We quit talking about money and started talking about life. By the next day, he was in treatment. And, thank God, he has begun a new life.

That young man wanted so desperately to pull the wool over my eyes, to dance the blind dance of death. He wanted that money and that fix so bad. But when the wool wouldn't be pulled, my young friend was forced to stop dancing, to stop squirming, to open his eyes, and to look inside with a wool-free gaze. As Pascal put it,

> If we could face ourselves, with all our faults, we would then be so shaken out of complacency, triviality, indifference, and pretense that a deep longing for strength and truth would be aroused within us. Not until man is aware of his

deepest need is he ready to discern and grasp what can meet that need.

I invite you to read on. I am most anxious that you discover "what can meet that need." But wiggling, wriggling, dancing, and wool-pulling must be set aside. Let's take an honest look within.

 **Chapter 3**

God, Can We Talk?

Who can say, "I have kept my heart pure; I am clean and without sin"?
Proverbs 20:9

The call to perfection before God is an assault on human reason. We find ourselves face-to-face with a demanding God, and there is no reasonable way out of it. It cannot be rationalized. But rationalize we will. We must, for our lives are at stake.

Has every possible human problem, foible, and addiction been rationalized during a talk-show segment in the past month-and-a-half? If not, I'm sure there are researchers scouring our highways and byways to deliver up the latest hodgepodge to Phil or Geraldo or Joan or Sally or Oprah. Joan Rivers has the motto to end all mottos for these programs: "Can we talk?"

In the search for perfection before God, there is an ongoing desire to talk, to rationalize all the details, to go through it over and over and over again. The desired goal of these rationalizations is to get off the hook. We humans have a great belief in the capacity of our minds to solve problems. As overwhelming as our problem with God and his demands, so much stronger is our confidence in our mental capacity. If we can talk it through long enough, the solution will appear, or maybe the problem will just go away. Consider with me now some of the ways we attempt to talk it through, to rationalize the demands of God.

No Neutral Corner

My family and I recently had the opportunity to visit Switzerland. Our tour guide explained the Swiss government's longstanding practice of neutrality. It turns out that it wasn't the way I had pictured it—the Swiss just throwing their hands up in the air, waving a white flag and yelling, "We're in the free zone," like kids in a game after dark. Being neutral means intense negotiations and a shrewd knowledge of politics and local mountain lore. The Swiss pull it off.

When it comes to a confrontation with the living God, neutrality is not an option. We cannot be Swiss, no matter how hard we try. If you have read this far, and you are not sure whether you even believe in God, you are probably pleading the case this way:

"Listen, everything you've said so far applies to religious types, those who care about God, those who need to find meaning in life through a personal encounter with a God. That is not me. I don't have to prove I'm perfect because I'm not involved with God. You can just leave me out."

There is a Peanuts cartoon in which Charlie Brown paraphrases Matthew 5:45 to Lucy: "The rain falls upon the just and the unjust." Lucy fixes him with an odd stare and replies, "That's some lousy system." But it is the system. And it applies here. Your belief or nonbelief in God in no way limits God's demand upon you. God is at work among believers and unbelievers—the "just" and the "unjust."

Martin Luther, speaking about the bondage of the human will to its own desires, said, "Bear in mind how incessantly active God is in all his creatures, allowing none of them to keep holiday." You are not allowed to limit God. And you do not get a vacation from God. Just because you are on the fence about God's existence does not mean that you are in a neutral corner. It just means you think you are hiding out, bobbing and weaving, shadowboxing, pretending no one can see you. In fact, however, you are in the middle of the ring and a thunderous right hook is about to land on your chin.

On the other hand, over in the corner sit religious folks thinking smugly, "About time for some hellfire and brimstone; judgment and damnation.

Thank goodness I don't have to worry about it anymore; I'm saved. I made my decision for Jesus. I'm off the hook. Put the screws to those unbelievers."

But remember how the system works. "The rain falls upon the just and the unjust." God's demand for perfection remains in place as long as the rains continue to fall—which for you will be as long as you live. If you have given up all sinning and become totally good—even perfect—then chuck off your shoes and flap your wings and fly off to heaven. If not, then you have lost your claim to neutrality. You are not Swiss. You are in this discussion for the long haul.

We Claim Cultural Conditioning

Reason resides in many cranial corners. Another rational appeal to overcome God's demand for perfection is to claim cultural conditioning. "Hold on," say our anthropologist types. "The Japanese have a different idea of what's perfect from Americans. Just check out the upkeep on my Honda compared to your Pontiac. Different cultures and groups of people are going to have different ideas of right and wrong, so there is no way to come up with a set of rules to measure perfection. 'Be ye therefore perfect' means different things to different people."

To this my response is, "Yes, but." In the New York City boroughs of Brooklyn and Queens there are 97 distinct cultural and racial groups speaking

67 languages. That is fact. Yes, there are differences, some gigantic, across cultures. But beneath all cultural and tribal divisions there is a unity. *All* have "oughts."

Every culture produces for individuals a way to evaluate what they are doing. And you are checked off by outside authority even as you check it off inside yourself—"I did good" or "I did bad," "I was right" or "I was wrong." This is undeniably imbedded in every culture. The Apostle Paul describes this process in an individual as the "thoughts now accusing, now even defending" (Romans 2:15). To put it simply, everyone has a conscience. Or, if you find someone who does not seem to have a conscience, you tell that person he or she better get one.

To take it a step further, that conscience of yours normally works to let you know when you have fallen short of external or internal standards. Then you begin to make your excuses. Why? Because you feel guilty. And you are worried. Because you have to face the facts, and the facts are not in your favor. And there are penalties—apologies, acts of making up—which you must begin to undertake. All cultures have "oughts" that lead to the conscience. There is no reasonable way of escaping it, whether you are Jew or Greek, Haitian or Dominican, German or American Indian. What you ought to have done before God, that you have not.

"Clean Enough," We Say

When I lived in a dormitory, my roommates and I developed a certain way of cleaning our room. About every month we would scour the place from top to bottom—under beds, behind mirrors, deep in the recesses of the closet—everywhere. Whatever we found we tossed into a pile. Then we moved that pile to the edge of the room. We added to it as the weeks wore on.

Visitors would pop in and we would pop off, "How about old P-303? This room gleams, doesn't it?" And the buddies would agree—until they saw the massive pile lurking over there in the corner. "What in the world is that?" they would ask nervously. "Oh, that," we would respond. "That's our mess. Don't go near that; it might be alive. But the *rest* of the room—doesn't it sparkle?"

When it comes to God's call to perfection, *all* the corners in *every* room of that cozy house called you have to be clean. Of course, this leads to fudging: Sweeping dust under the carpet. Creating a "junk room" with a big padlock on it.

No hiding places before God! Everything is available for inspection. Are you anxious for God's relentless expedition into the inner recesses of your being? Do you desire the analysis of your dos and don'ts through the eyes of Almighty God? I didn't think so. Who would? So you do what you do at home when guests come. You show off the master bedroom, the living room, and the kitchen.

And you put locks on the kids' rooms and the basement. This is not unusual.

Intellectuals, philosophers, and theologians through the centuries have tried to do the same thing when considering human imperfection in the gaze of a perfect God. "Look," they reason, "we are all God's creation. There has to be much that is good about us, because God doesn't make junk. So when God looks for perfection, He examines only a part of each of us. It is a serious part, a deep part, a 'soul' part. But it is only part. You would not condemn the whole house because the basement was a mess, would you?"

There are several serious problems with this argument. First, if the basement were in bad enough condition, you *might* condemn the whole house. I have certainly seen it in Brooklyn. Second, when it comes to you, the home is more than the sum of its rooms. There is no way to pick and pull you apart into soul, body, spirit, nerve endings, brainpan, and teeth. You are you, in total, a person before God. If your tooth aches, *you* ache. If there is uncleanness, imperfection before God in any part of you, then *you* are imperfect, *you* are unclean.

The Bible says, "O Lord, you have searched me and you know me. You know when I sit and when I rise; you perceive my thoughts from afar. ... Before a word is on my tongue you know it completely, O Lord" (Psalm 139:1–2, 4). *All* of you is known by God. All of you is under his consideration, his inspection, his requirements, his demands.

Psychologists, of course, say this is not healthy. Why would religious types like me run around telling everybody they are unclean? (I'm not just saying that people have unclean areas in them; this would be readily admitted. What I am saying is that people are *by nature* unclean; the entire *being* of every person is affected.) This does not seem to promote mental health. This could lead to an overwhelming sense of guilt and powerlessness. Many in our psychologically oriented, power-oriented society oppose not only the awareness of a fatally flawed human nature but along with it the search for perfection before God and underneath it the very existence of God.

But if what we are discussing is true, it would lead to a level of awareness deeper by far than the deepest depth psychology, would it not? You would be forced to admit that no matter how many mental blocks were removed, no matter how well you came to grips with the way you were toilet trained, no matter how many specific problems and mistakes you analyzed and wiped away, you could never catch up. There are dark corridors beyond prowling, hidden chasms that elude all inner vision, vulnerable spots inside you beyond denial.

Excuses Are Useless

Beneath all rationalization, a certain very real word is lurking. That word is *payback*. As an ancient aphorism explains, "Whatever you sow, that shall you reap." (Also check out Galatians 6:7.) In contemporary terms, "What goes around comes around." This is the law of retribution. It is a universal constant. It applies to each and all, from street hoodlums to corporate queens and kings to sanitation engineers.

If you think about payback too much, you will begin to feel terrified, since the one who holds you in an eternal position of retributive payback is God. So let's back off for a moment.

"What," you ask, "does this prove? Just because we all have a conscience and there exists a kind of internal check-off system telling me that I am in permanent debt, that doesn't prove there's a *God* out there demanding perfection. You're just describing the human creative impulse. You're simply talking about people around the globe organizing their lives and societies the best way they can. We are still the masters of our own destinies. We remain our own last best hope."

To this my reply is, "You may choose to think so." The Masters of Destiny category is better left to hulking Saturday morning cartoon characters than to human beings. What we human beings have been good at through the centuries is wars and rumors of war. What goes around comes around—and around and around. The conscience continues to call you to a destiny you cannot reach, to terms you cannot fulfill, to do what you cannot begin to do, and to refrain from doing that which you cannot seem to stop doing. I am contending that God is behind this process.

And I am contending that God demands payback. God demands in retribution what is God's: your *life*.

 **Chapter 4**

Rose-Colored Glasses

What good will it be for a man if he gains the whole world, yet forfeits his soul? Matthew 16:26

T he question has become, Are you getting better and better? Could you meet God face-to-face on an equal basis? Are you up to that task? Remember, you are called to be better than better; you must be perfect.

"Relentlessly upbeat"—a friend of mine has been described that way. For her, the cup is neither half-empty nor half-full. It is always overflowing. Do you know the kind of person I'm talking about? She looks at life through rose-colored glasses. Much of the time I want to say, "More power to you." In a beat-up world, it is good to find someone who is upbeat. But is she for real? And, more importantly, is she right? Are things rosy?

American society is hard-driving, fast-paced.

We are a people on the move, on the grow. Some-times to observers, to those from other parts of the world who watch our TV shows, who see us shopping in the malls, who sit in the bleachers at our games, we seem to be relentlessly upbeat. We smile on cue, peering at our stop 'n' shoot cameras. Why not? After all, that pose might make "America's Funniest Home Videos." In truth, my happy-go-lucky friend and all of us have been well-trained by both philosophers and advertisers to look at life through rose-colored glasses.

In the past two chapters I have shown how an examination of the attitudes of the heart and the mind reveals our helplessness before the demands of God. In this chapter, we will be treating some of society's attitudes that attempt to pry us off the hook before God.

We Try Rose-Colored Glasses

For a long time, roughly since the Revolutionary War, some thinkers have insisted that "things are getting better and better." Cars, planes, inoculations, x-rays, VCRs, and cellular phones are all trotted out in support. These are the important "advances." Slowly but surely we are living longer, living better, living in a more civilized way—the enlightened progressives reason. It is an enticing point of view because, really, are any of us interested in going back before the dawn of time when you couldn't tape your favorite show, when granny picked and cooked all meals from scratch, when a man might have one suit, a woman a couple of dresses, when polio and smallpox were killers, when (horror of horrors) there were no shopping malls?

Yet even as the computer prints out recipes for the microwave and cellular telephones beep in happy reply, the way we act, our moral behavior, continues its steep decline. Nazi Germany, the H-bomb, Vietnam, Cambodia, and nerve gas stand as horrible proof that things are not getting better, at least not in this century. Nor are we. An outbreak of democracy in Eastern Europe, 1989, is followed by an outbreak of aggression in the Middle East, 1990. The hungry keep dying, and the planet's resources keep shrinking.

The "things are getting better and better" philosophers assumed that all the fine ideas and inventions would be put to fine and inventive use by fine and inventive leaders. In this way the fine and creative forces of humanity would be in control of our human destiny. At a deeper level is the belief that ideas would win the day. By knowing more about ourselves and the world around us, we would gain the measure of our future place on the planet.

Not to put a damper on anyone's optimism, but let's be real! We live impolitely on planet earth—quite impolitely. Our destiny is most definitely in doubt.

Besides, even if you happen to be living in a beachfront condo in sunny Boca Raton, you cannot dodge the issue by saying "things are getting better and better." In fact, even if world-wide lasting peace were to break out tomorrow and everyone were as polite as could be, the question would still require an answer.

The question is this: Are *you* getting better and better? Could *you* meet God face-to-face on an equal basis? Are *you* up to that task? Remember, *you* are called to be better than better. *You* must be *perfect*.

When Jesus says, "Be ye therefore perfect," you are not allowed to show him your mint-condition 1956 Mickey Mantle baseball card and claim the perfection of its condition. Nor are you allowed to show him the garden-fresh bud from your finest rose bush, sparkling with dewy perfection. No, it is the perfection of your condition before God that is required. And, gazing at you through my word processor, that most modern communication tool, I can say it frankly: You are looking more than a little peaked. You definitely do not look rosy.

We Try "Love"

Enlightened philosophers may not be your cup of tea. You may be a hardened realist when it comes to global politics and trends. But there are other, more basic thought patterns out there influencing you to swing according to their sway. Like love.

New York is the home of the Long Island Expressway, also known as the world's longest parking lot. Rush hour is crush hour and it's four hours long. For me (and about two million other New York drivers) it is absolutely mandatory to know the shortcuts. Side streets, alleys, double-loop exits, quick off and back on, these are the stock in trade of every driver worth her or his salt in the Big Apple. Save a minute, jump a car length, find a secret route—these are the victories we live for.

There are no such shortcuts when dealing with God. There is no cheap victory. There is no back road home. God must be faced on God's terms.

Do you want to know a shortcut almost everyone tries? (I know I have.) It is the shortcut of love. And this is how it goes:

God is love
> **THEREFORE** God loves everything
> I am part of everything
> **THEREFORE** God loves me

> **GRAND THEREFORE:** *What, me worry?*

This may sound familiar. I know I have been pulled into this particular conversation on factory assembly lines, on street corners, at church meetings, and after softball games. This very common discussion about God is, on the surface, very biblical. "God *is* love," says 1 John 4:8—and we all believe in love, if not in God. So we are on familiar ground here. We date, marry, work, give birth, shop, drive, smoke, refrain from smoking, eat, refrain from eating, and purchase cemetery plots all for love. It is our code word for the deep things, the heartfelt things, the innermost things. *Love.* And we discover from the Bible that God is love. Perfect. That completes the circle. We are about love and God is about love. So everything is rosy once again.

There is just one word of warning: Beware the thorns. I know this will be a problem, because the thorns are *you*. *God* is love: this is most certainly true. But you—are *you* love? Am I love? Don Matzat wrote a whole book on the fallacy of the self-esteem movement that has swept the country. "Humanistic psychology," he says, teaches "that each individual person is responsible and is able to take control of his own life. He is able to find himself and *feel good about himself*" (*Christ-Esteem* [Eugene, OR; Harvest House Publishers, Inc.; 1990]). Self-esteem leads by simple necessity to failure, to despair. Self-esteem is a way to avoid the thorny truth. In fact, it is triply thorny.

First of all, the thorny truth about us is that the perfect love of God only scrapes away the paint on my imperfect love. I do not live up to any kind of standards of love-ability, neither toward God nor toward my wife and pets. Do you? Are you *always* "there" for whomever or whatever comes first on your earthly love list? If a major-league baseball player gets a hit once for every three times at the plate, he is headed for the Hall of Fame. That's about my batting average when it comes to earthly love—.333. Maybe you're better than I am—say a .500 performer, a candidate for the Love Hall of Fame. Maybe you're among the all-time greats and you love all things and all people 87½ percent of the time. You're amazing!

God, friends, is batting 1.000. Always has. Always will. So our talking about our marvelous love performance does not make our love perfect. In fact, the longer we talk, the less lovely we sound.

Second, even if we grant that love is something we can consider on a human scale—I *do* love my wife, I *can* love a sunset over Manhattan from the Brooklyn promenade or out in the magnificent Rockies—does this mean that I can love God?

The answer is "yes, in my way." The trouble is, "in my way" has oceans to do with what is in it for me. What passes for love on this planet really has to do with personal satisfaction, personal pleasure, what is in it for me. "What is in it for me" when it comes to loving God is that I want God to love me back, bless me, give me what I need/want/ deserve, and dance to my tune. Is this quality love? Is this real love?

This element of self-satisfaction is a basic component of all human love, and this is the reason we cannot in fact love God. Our love is turned in on itself, on the unloveliness in us. Therefore, it cannot satisfy. When I begin the process of serious self-evaluation, I run into a very unlovely realization. "I know that nothing good lives in me"

(Romans 7:18). We cannot invent a shortcut through the thicket of the human heart to God and his true love. We are stuck on the thorns of our own ingrown desires.

The third thorn of the truth about ourselves is that we take great pains to dress up God in *our* ideology of love: God is love—therefore everybody is off the hook. After all, we reason, true love overlooks imperfections. In fact, true love is blind to imperfections. How else could my wife have married me? If Judy did it, then God also has to take me as I am.

Now without jumping the gun too much on what lies ahead, let me simply say this: Yes, God does love you as you are. But he does not love you because you want it that way; he does not love you because somehow you get to make God's decision about you for him.

That line of argumentation is as old as the hills. My mom used to set spinach in front of me when company came and I couldn't talk back, and she'd smile so nice and say, "David just loves his spinach." And I'd choke it down, thinking, "It's bad enough I've got to eat this seaweed without her telling everybody I love it!"

How much more would God in heaven choke on the love we would try to push down his throat. We do *not* get to tell God that God is required to love us. It is as simple as that. Otherwise we would have power over God and we would be as God. This is the essence of arrogance. That is where all the trouble began back in the garden at that one particular tree where the first couple, egged on by their wriggly buddy, thought they could bite right into the knowledge of good and evil and become as their Maker.

No—God is love, and we are not. The thorns choke the Rose.

We Try Bettering Ourselves

If neither the high roads of enlightened philosophy nor Love Potion Number 9 can steer us clear of God's demands, maybe good old American salesmanship will restore those rosy cheeks and that big sunshine smile as you encounter God.

Here's the windup and the pitch: "Hey, come on, smile! Wipe off that frown—I know you can do it! There you go. And wouldn't that smile look so much better if you brushed your teeth with Colgate? Just happen to have a tube with me, for a mere $2.89." Strike one!

Some of my favorite people in the world are salespeople. I'm kind of funny that way. Maybe it's because they remind me of me. I'm often thumping the tub as I hawk salvation like a heavenly medicine man. At least that's the way many people see me. And it rubs off. Salespeople, you see, are great examples of the value our society places on knowing yourself and believing in yourself. You've got to keep your sunny side up to sell pots and pans.

The salesperson who doesn't believe in herself or himself, even if the product is wonderful, is going to end up with a pile of vacuum cleaners in the trunk of the car. Those salespeople who don't believe in themselves, who don't know themselves, their strengths and weaknesses, can't get ahead. They get left behind.

Nobody wants to get left behind. Things are moving so fast. We all want to get ahead. One of the great indicators of our unquenchable thirst to get ahead is the enormous amount of time, energy, and money we pour into self-help and motivational media—books, videos, tapes, lectures, courses, retreats, info-tainment TV shows, and seminars— all of it. You need to know how to get ahead—and you need to know now!

If you work for a progressive corporation, you will probably receive motivational training from some super-salesperson who charges megabucks for prepackaged words of wisdom. Sure, it's going to mean bigger profits for the corporation, which, by the way, benefit you; but really you are the one who's going to live better, smarter, more profitably. Have you heard this pitch at work? If not, then some night when you can't fall asleep, turn on one of those off-network channels and catch the masters of manipulation after midnight doing their stuff, offering you for only $39.95 a 90-minute instructional video that will restore self-confidence, heal boils and blisters, and guarantee you an annual income in excess of $600,000, if only you'll learn to "believe in yourself."

I, too, am concerned that you get ahead. I am

concerned enough to be talking with you about the most important, most powerful relationship in your life; your relationship with the living God.

I want you to get ahead with God.

You go to church. You have begun to read this book. You have an incurable interest in being all that you can be, up to and including the way you relate to God. You may be holding a position of leadership in a Christian congregation.

There are two necessary ingredients for you to get ahead. You must know and believe in God as God truly is. And you must know yourself as you truly are. That is what it's going to take to get ahead with God.

Now I have already told you one truth about you and one about God. These truths have come directly from the mouth of Jesus: "Be ye therefore perfect, even as your Father which is in heaven is perfect" (Matthew 5:48 KJV).

Jesus demands that you examine yourself thoroughly. How well do you know yourself? How much do you believe in yourself?

These questions are serious, no sales pitch included. They deserve serious consideration. We do not live in a society that encourages the serious consideration of life's ultimate meaning. We are sold "soft soap" at every commercial break. Who deserves a break today? You do, of course. Who says so? McDonald's, of course. Seventy-five billion burgers sold.

Let me emphasize the need to take off the rose-colored glasses. Let me emphasize the need to see the world, to see your world, as it is. Let me emphasize the need for honesty. Let me emphasize the need to beware the thorns. Let me emphasize the simple words of Jesus:

"What good will it be for a man if he gains the whole world, yet forfeits his soul?" (Matthew 16:26).

 **Chapter 5**

Put It in Writing

*So then, the law is holy, and the com-
mandment is holy, righteous and good.
Romans 7:12*

How special are we? We are so special that
we get a special deal, a special arrangement. Rules have been made and written that
apply only to us, which bind only humans to God.
That's how special we are.

It is time we got something in writing. We have
motored down the road in this headlong journey
toward a meeting of destiny, an encounter with the
living God. But we have been moving without any
written guidelines, without a road map, so to
speak. Certainly the inner testimony of heart and
mind suggest strongly that there is a God who
holds all accountable. But there is more. What I
wish to tell you now is that not only are the
demands of God inscribed upon your heart, your
mind, and your conscience, there is also a written

document on which is engraved God's truth for all generations. Our internal journey needs external witness.

God has provided. The written ledger is the Holy Bible, a book of 66 books divided into two sections. The ledger we will open first is called the Law, the so-called Books of Moses, but it is also part and parcel of the entire document.

Can this book be trusted? Is it reliable? Is it true? My answer is a resounding yes. It is true to itself; it is reliable in describing not only events but also the foundations of reality. At its most basic level it will accomplish for any reader what it promises. It will lead you to meet the living God at all the levels of disclosure God permits.

How do you know God? You by yourself are severely limited by your inner impressions or the impressions of a few friends. The right way to get to know anybody—and especially God—is to learn what he says about himself. As Martin Luther put it long ago, "We have to do with God as clothed and displayed in his Word, by which he presents himself to us. That is his glory and beauty."

People have been throwing mud on God's garment for some time now. Well-respected biblical scholars have taken the blue pencil to almost anything Jesus said in the gospels. These scholars indicate that Jesus never spoke the words; rather, later authors and editors put them in his mouth. Recent volumes treat the work of Matthew, Mark, Luke, and John as literary art—not fact, but fiction.

If God reveals himself to us most clearly through Jesus the Messiah, God's only begotten Son, then we must be able to trust the record of his life in the Bible or we are in deep trouble. The Word of God is not simply the imagination of some well-meaning 2,000-year-old creative geniuses. If this were so, I'd rather settle down with an Agatha Christie mystery or the latest National Geographic. There is no glory, no beauty left in the Word.

Of course, it is not so. For our sake, the Word of God remains God's beautiful garment. The Word is precious beyond measure, because it reveals us as we truly are and also reveals God's sure promise made perfect for us in Jesus Christ. Trust the Word!

Ordered by the Law

One of the favorite gimmicks used in science-fiction movies is the "invisible force field." The good guys are scooting down a tunnel to escape the alien warriors. They see light. They're almost out—then WHONK! They've run headlong into The Invisible Force Field! Oh, no! They feel their way up and down the field like pantomime artists. Then someone throws a switch, and the field appears in all its electric fury. The sparks become an unconquerable prison wall. Our heroes are trapped, they're sunk. If only Spock had thought to bring the de-energizer. But wait—there's still hope!

There is such a spiritual force field, friends. It exists. It is infinitely more than a gimmick to excite fans of the USS Enterprise and its crew. It is the very order of the universe. It is God's order of the universe. It is called the Law.

The Law of God is powerful and mighty. It can be visible or invisible to human observers. It organizes and orchestrates the ways human beings relate to God, to one another, and to the world. Yet in the end, same as for our interplanetary heroes, the force field called the Law puts us in fatal jeopardy. By now, you have felt the shocks of this force field. As we have considered God's call to perfection, you have bumped up against the wall every which way. It hurt each time. Now the force field is going to be revealed. The Law of God will become apparent to you. Maybe the best advice I can give you is, "Look out!"

You live under the Law of God, his divine order of the universe. But you knew that, at least in part. Some laws you see, some you assume. Take the law of gravity. You don't see it, but it's there. Sure, if you're Galileo, Mr. Wizard, or a member of the high school science project team, you can set up some experiment to prove the invisible force field called gravity. But basically all you have to do is jump. When you jump, do you fall up or down? Gravity is a "law" because it always applies everywhere. You don't have a choice when it comes to gravity—you don't "do" gravity. It "does" you.

We have been placed into a world ordered with laws, with fields of force such as gravity. The Law is the way we are connected to our past, to our

biology, to the world around us. Jesus links us with the "birds of the air" and invites us to "see how the lilies of the field grow" (Matthew 6:26, 28). We are part of that divine order, that arrangement, that deal. We are under the Law, just like the birds of the air and the fish of the sea. This isn't too painful, is it? So far you're jumping in the fields with the birds and bees. As Jesus compares us to the animal and vegetable kingdom in Matthew 6, he asks, "Are you not much more valuable than they?" It is a word of comfort—sort of. The answer is, "Yes, we are more valuable." Why? Because that is the way God made us. We are special inside the order of God's Law. In Psalm 8 the author thanks God when considering humankind because "you made him a little lower than the heavenly beings and crowned him with glory and honor."

How special are we? We are so special that we get a special deal, a special arrangement. Rules have been made and written that apply only to us, which bind only humans to God. That is how special we are.

Do I hear an "uh-oh" escaping your lips? Do I feel some sparks flying from the force field? Is that you, trying to jump the fence while you can? Don't worry. You can climb that wall as long as—and I think by now you know what's coming—you are perfect.

Playing by the Rules

I'm standing at my doorway when a pink rubber ball bonks me on the bean. Better watch out, the neighborhood kids are playing stickball. What they're actually doing is having a two-hour argument during which a stickball game breaks out every now and then.

"Ball one."

"Ball—no way; that was a strike! It hit the corner!"

"What corner? Home plate is a manhole cover—it's a circle!"

"Fair ball—hit the bumper on the Chevy."

"Foul—foul. Cars are foul territory."

"Not the Chevy; he's parked too far from the curb. That bumper is fair!"

When the pavement sizzles in summer, this goes on endlessly, from dawn to midnight.

Once I went out to make peace, being a clergyman and therefore a professional manager of conflict, and a former ballplayer to boot. "Guys," I ventured, "your problem is you keep changing the rules. Why don't you write 'em down and have a copy handy. Then you've got it in black and white. No need to argue."

They looked at me as though I had just landed from Mars. Then they began to laugh in whoops and gales, falling down in the street. I was half afraid they'd get hit by passing traffic.

"Write it down!" they surrounded me in derision. "What, are you kidding? We know these rules like the back of our hand. Write 'em down? Oh, man, that's a good one!"

They continued to laugh at my suggestion and to argue from dawn to dusk—until they turned fourteen and began chasing members of the opposite sex instead of balls. No matter. Their places were filled immediately by another troop of ten-year-olds. Same rules. Same arguments. Like big leaguers with their contracts, the kids of the Brooklyn streets are learning that the negotiations are the essence of the game.

We are all that way, really. Negotiations form a major part of every daily interaction with spouse and (particularly) children. We love to set the terms, make the deal, negotiate from strength, make the sharpest settlement. You have to make some arrangements, make some deals with one another, in order to know where you stand, to keep things clean and well-organized.

Covenant Agreement

So we have the Law of God as a written code. We have the letter of the Law. And, as St. Paul said, "The law is holy, and the commandment is holy, righteous and good" (Romans 7:12). Without the Law, we would not know the boundaries, where the Chevy ends and the curb begins, what is fair and what is foul. We would not know what God demands. We would not know the terms of the deal. Now I'm going to let you in on some inside information. There is one extremely important thing to know about the deal God makes through the Law: he sets the terms.

The Ten Commandments form a basic part of that written Law. Once we have acknowledged the boundary they form, we can try to stay inside of it. Since the Law is holy and pure and comes from God, if we always make our home inside its perfect bounds we will be considered perfect. The written code, therefore, holds the promise of life with God. Even though we did not get to write or approve the basics, this is not such a bad deal. Indeed, God said on Mount Sinai, "If you obey me ... you will be my treasured possession" (Exodus 19:5).

We all learn to make deals in this way. If you have ever purchased a home, do you remember how your John Hancock squirted all over the page? Just as pen hit paper you realized that you were making a deal to find and designate skatey-eight percent of your monthly income to some bank for the next 30 years of your life, come rain or shine, be you just or unjust. You realized then that that lousy bumper sticker—the one that reads "I Owe, I Owe, It's Off to Work I Go"—might as well be glued to your forehead. You signed on the dotted line. And now you have to pay.

The Law of God is the written form of just such an agreement. To live under its terms is one way to be called "righteous." But is it really possible to live up perfectly to all the terms of the agreement?

If so, maybe all the arguments of conscience and mental process we have waded through so far can be chucked down the chute. Maybe the written Law, the deal done in black and white, is the only way out.

But one more question lurks in the background (now that we are busy viewing the Law as the deal that describes the way we relate to God): "What is the bottom line? If I fail to live up to the written terms, what are my penalties? What is at stake?"

 **Chapter 6**

The Letter of the Law

The sting of death is sin, and the power of sin is the law. 1 Corinthians 15:56

The letter of the Law pins us, all of us, every one of us. The Apostle Paul puts it very simply, "The letter kills" (2 Corinthians 3:6). Whom does it kill? All who must live up to it. You cannot live up to the terms of the agreement. There is no way out.

Let us enter the world of rules and regulations. Let us enter the world of the letter of the law.

Have you ever run up against your municipality's building, health, or fire codes? These rules must be followed to the letter. Serving as pastor of a church and executive director of a church-run day-care center, I have had many encounters at our facility with the legions of code inspectors who keep New York City obedient to the letter.

Recently, the buzzer rang and one of the feared inspectors entered the church property. A code blue alarm went off in my head. He stood just inside the door, and we had this little chat:

Me: Good morning, fine sir. What a pleasant surprise! If I knew you were coming, I'd have baked a cake—ha, ha! Well, no matter that you couldn't call ahead to make an appointment. I'm sure you will find everything shipshape.

Inspector: The lock affixed to the fire door entranceway through which I just passed is of a dead bolt nature. You are in violation of fire code 265-3B.

Me: I had no idea! What does this mean? [*I immediately plead ignorance before all code-book-toting inspectors.*]

Inspector: It means quite simply that if the dead bolt type lock is not removed before I exit these premises, your day-care center will be closed indefinitely. Health code 386-B1.

Me: Do you happen to have a screwdriver with you?

Inspector: No, I do not. However, upon entrance, I also noticed that your emergency lighting system contains bulbage installed at requisite distance intervals further than lighting code 490-2A permits, namely, 24 feet, 8 inches.

Me: Ah, I hadn't noticed that. [*Now he's got me thinking: (a) What in the world is* bulbage? *Is that a word? (b) This man has amazing eyesight! He can determine the difference between lights installed 25 feet apart and 24 feet, 8 inches, at a glance! (c) That four-inch difference will cost my operation $6,000 for new electrical wiring.*]

Inspector: Overhead, your illuminated exit sign is functioning at a wattage level below the tolerance required in illumination/exit code 871-W. If further baso-wattage exit function exists at other egress points, complete reinstallation procedures must be undertaken.

Me: I guess we're just not too bright! Ha, ha. Just a little humor. [*I'm now mulling it over internally: Do I have a relative who's an electrician? This is going to amount to some big bucks.*]

Inspector: This is no laughing matter. I have barely entered your building, and already four major violations have been uncovered—including the fact that your certificate of occupancy sign is affixed to the improper wall at a height not deemed optimum, as required in building code 1098745-62:H.

Me: Be assured, sir, that I am not laughing on the inside. [*How can I let this rule-bound step another foot deeper into my violation-ridden premises?*]

On such a day, I would weep for joy if there were only 10 building commandments in New York City. I would gladly become a Pharisee or even a Publican if there were only 613 demands to obey in addition to the basic 10 in order to be counted righteous before the city fathers. No, if you put the building, health, and fire codes together, there may be 50–to 100–million rules to follow. At least that's the way it feels. Failure to live up to the letter of the law can put you behind the eight ball and on the *fine* line (that's the endless line in which you stand to pay fines).

The letter of the law has become a book thousands of times longer than *War and Peace*. Building codes, health codes, fire codes, tenant law, motor vehicle licensing, marriage law, environmental law, the IRS and tax law, and when you die, surrogate law for your will and/or bequest. And we're not even talking about the criminal level. When it comes to law, we're all lettered up.

No Loopholes

The Law of God is also to be followed to the letter. It has always been that way, and it is not going to change, according to Jesus. He knew that to shift a few words would eliminate penalties and allow loopholes to appear. Some folks thought maybe he had come to let them off the hook, to destroy the system, and usher in a kinder, gentler time. "Sorry," he said in no uncertain terms. "It is easier for heaven and earth to disappear than for the least stroke of a pen do drop out of the Law" (Luke 16:17). There are no loopholes in the entire letter of the Law, the whole volume.

Jesus attacked those who treated the letter of the Law lightly. He wanted people to know it is not about externals. It is not about the fine print. It is about your heart. "For out of the heart come evil thoughts, murder, adultery, sexual immorality, theft, false testimony, slander" (Matthew 15:19). You cannot hide around the edges of the letter of the Law. It does not protect; it exposes. The letter is not for the surface; it is for the depths. It is not about the posting of some certificate of occupancy on the proper wall; it is about you, the occupant. It is about your heart, your soul, your spirit before the living God.

Do me a favor. Try a simple exercise. Read the Ten Commandments. It won't take long. There are only 10. Now do what Jesus tells us to do. Take them to heart. Remember, there are no loopholes. "You shall not murder," Jesus reminds us, refers not only to teen-age gun toters. In the realm of the heart, it goes to intent—to anger, to the desire to harm another human being. How do you stand?

Now try "You shall not commit adultery." In the realm of the heart, it goes to intent—to the desire for another person outside marriage.

Move on down the line. How about "You shall not give false testimony against your neighbor"? It goes to the heart, to the desire to damage someone else's reputation, or to listen to the gossip that makes someone else smaller because you feel somehow larger. How big are your britches?

The list goes on. (I'm saving the toughest, the First Commandment, for later.) And once the letter of the Law penetrates the heart, there is no room for imperfection, is there? But examine your heart. Consider all the people you have hurt. Consider how you have hurt, damaged, and maimed your own integrity. "There is no one righteous, not even one" (Romans 3:10).

The letter of the Law pins us, all of us, every one of us. The Apostle Paul put it very simply: "The letter kills." Whom does it kill? All who must live up to it. You cannot live up to the terms of the agreement. There is no way out.

No Way Out

I had a meeting once in the World Trade Center. It is, to both tourist and resident, awesomely enormous. There is sufficient concrete in its structures to build a two-lane highway to the moon. On my way to the meeting, I get stuck in New York traffic, so I have to park in the lot under the Trade Center's 1,200-foot-high Twin Towers. I do mean under. There are about half as many stories underground as the hundred plus above. Down under they are all filled with cars. It's kind of purgatory's parking lot, sunk down there about one gray, exhaust-filled level above fire and brimstone. That's the feeling.

So I wend my way through the maze down to

level 14. I park the car and head for the elevator. And get lost. Completely, thoroughly lost.

I begin to walk from aisle to aisle, from massive pillar to monumental post, looking for a way out. There is none.

"Aha!" I reason, breathing hard, talking to myself now. "I'll head for a wall and find a door and walk up. Fourteen floors back up to the world. I can do it."

I'm a pretty smart individual, really, especially when I'm petrified. Fear sparks the brain cells. Eventually I find a door. It is locked. The door is locked!

About 15 minutes later I am still lost, my heart pumping like a piston. The walls are closing in on me. The incredible weight of the Twin Towers is pressing on my neck. I can't breathe!

Then, finally, another car rolls in. I'm sure to this day the driver remembers me, a wild-eyed maniac banging on his hood, shouting, "Help me! Help me! I have to get out of here! I'm trapped!"

I definitely remember him, slowly rolling down his window, peering out at me, looking beyond me for police protection, then uttering the words of my salvation, "Hey, pal, relax! The elevator's right there. Next to you. You're leaning against it, for crying out loud. Just press the button. And relax! You look terrible!"

At least I had an exit.

The Commandments stand like pillars and beams. The regulations can get you running like a rat in a maze. And finally when you turn the last corner, you become this wild-eyed creature banging on the walls, up against that invisible force field begging to be let out. But there is no exit. When it comes to the letter of the Law, the Law of God hems you in.

Read the letter, written down in the Bible: "Now we know that whatever the law says, it says to those who are under the law, so that every mouth may be silenced and the whole world held accountable to God. Therefore no one will be declared righteous in his sight by observing the law; rather, through the law we become conscious of sin" (Romans 3:19–20). "The soul who sins is the one who will die" (Ezekiel 18:4). "Cursed is everyone who does not continue to do everything written in the Book of the Law" (Galatians 3:10).

The letter strikes you down. It is literally killing you. The sensation is like sitting in a small locked room with no roof in a thunderstorm. You've got nowhere to go and nothing to do but get wet and worried, and then—BANG—a bolt of lightning whacks you. As men once said, "This, then, is the thunderbolt of God by which he hurls to the ground both manifest sinners and hypocrites, and declares no one righteous, but drives them altogether to terror and despair."

All Are Trapped

Let me pause for a moment as this sinks in. The word *everyone* can be too generic, like the cans without labels on Safeway's bargain aisle. We need to get specific. We need to brand some names. When the Bible says everyone is cursed under the Law, that includes even the following: grandma and grandpa in the nursing home, junior in diapers, congressmen and convicted felons, little girls in white dresses, working class heroes and bums in the gutter, teenagers and tennis stars, big league athletes and beer-bellied slow-pitch softballers, Africans, North Americans, South Americans, Asians, Australians, Europeans, and residents of the islands worldwide, the nice and the nasty, addicts and abstainers, me and my family, and *you!*

The Law, God's thunderbolt, has knocked us all to the ground in terror and despair. Unless you understand the complete and utterly terminal magnitude of the problem, you will not be able to appreciate the depth of the riches and wisdom and love and tender mercy of God's solution. Nobody is off the hook. You must be perfect.

The call to perfection before God is an assault on human reason. We find ourselves face-to-face with a demanding God, and there is no reasonable way out of it. It cannot be rationalized. But rationalize we will. We must, for our lives are at stake.

 **Chapter 7**

The Enemy Is Us

What shall we say, then? Is the law sin?
Certainly not! Indeed I would not have
known what sin was except through the
law. Romans 7:7

Sin—you were born that way. You don't become a sinner by sinning. *You sin because you are a sinner.* It is you, as you are.

The Real You

Like me when I was trapped in the sub-sub-basement, we all come face-to-face with fear when our imperfections are exposed before God's Law. We are trapped by the rules, which lock us in a cage. But more to the point, we are trapped by ourselves, the desires of our own hearts—and that is truly frightening. All of us have been scared to death at one time or another. Some of you have fought inward battles; others have had to face sudden and tragic loss; still others live in homes with triple-locked doors and bars on the windows. You all know fear, and some know it far too well. I am talking to you now about a fear that, once you acknowledge it, will gnaw and bite at you like no other.

There is no comfort, no peace within when the Law accuses. And it will accuse. With fear and trembling, it is time for the real you to face the living God.

Have you ever used an industrial-strength floor sander? It will reveal a wood surface you never saw before. Several years ago our church's parish hall badly needed renovation. After 85 years, it was showing wear.

Made of hard red oak, these planks had felt the feet of the humble, the penitent, the proud, and the plain when the building was used for worship. Since those days, we played basketball on the hardwood and hosted thousands of tricycle rides for little ones. The floor was beat up, blackened, scarred. Then the sanding machines did their thing. Dust rose up as layer after layer of dirt and wax and varnish was peeled away. Finally after two days we reached wood. We discovered it was top-quality wood. Exposed to the light of the sun for the first time in decades, they gleamed and shone reddish white. The layers of time had been peeled away. The real wood was exposed to the sun.

Jesus, trained as a carpenter, was also a great sander. He could peel away the layers of a person's being until the soul stood exposed for all to see. Jesus had a running battle with the religious leaders of his day and culture. Finally, during the week of his death, he let them have it: "Woe to you, teachers of the law and Pharisees, you hypocrites! You are like whitewashed tombs, which look beautiful on the outside but on the inside are full of dead men's bones ... on the inside you are full of hypocrisy and wickedness" (Matthew 23:27, 28). Whoof! No more Mr. Nice Guy. This is certainly not gentle Jesus, meek and mild. He cuts to the bone.

We are exposed in exactly the same way. The Law of God sands and scrapes us all down to the same common level, planks on the same floor—except we're not top-quality wood; we have dry rot. The Law reveals us as sinners. As Paul said, "I would not have known what sin was except through the law." In the words of the Master, "Flesh gives birth to flesh" (John 3:6). It could not be otherwise. We all spring from the same source. We are all human. We all have proceeded from the world's original gardener and sinner, Adam.

So Who's to Blame?

This can lead to a lot of finger pointing. Originally it was God pointing at Adam: "What have you done?" Then Adam pointed to Eve and back at God: "It was the woman you gave me." Then Eve pointed to the serpent and to God: "It was that snake, the one you made." Now, 10 billion humans later, we could all end up pointing back through mom, dad, grandpa, and grandma unto the 3,748th generation, until all fingers are aimed and wagging at old Adam again. "It's his fault—he got me into this mess." We love to do this, don't we? Making excuses, fingering somebody way down the line. Especially if they are long dead and cannot defend themselves.

It will not wash. You still must hold up your end of the bargain personally. Martin Luther liked to call original sin "person sin." It is personally in you and in every person—"There is *no one* who does good, not even one" (Romans 3:12); "*All* have sinned" (Romans 3:23). The violent negative force of original sin sweeps through your head, your heart, your actions, and your attitudes every day. It is in the totality that is you, you in person. And you are held personally responsible. There are no excuses. Death is one proof. And death comes to your door, the apostle Paul says, because "all have sinned." Each and all. Individually. Personally.

Still, what could you do about it? You were born this way. Good excuse, right?

It's like my nose. I have been given by nature a particular proboscis. This accident of birth will be with me, unless I miss my guess, until death. Peering at yellowed photographs in the family archives, I have come to appreciate the truth of genetic inheritance. Bits and pieces of my own *nariz grande,* as they say in Spanish, dot (or fill) the centers of the faces of my ancestors from the third and fourth generation. When I was a kid, people used to tease me about my nose. "Hey, get a load of that beak!" Or, "Here's a beach towel, buddy. You can use it as a handkerchief." I was forced to consider my nose, the one my parents and their parents gave me. Through the years I've not only gotten used to it, I kind of like it. It breathes well. And if some neighborhood youths pause in their pursuits to inquire just where I acquired such an appendage, I jump in with, "Hey, fellas, I was born with it."

So it is with sin. You were born that way. You do not become a sinner by sinning, *you sin because you are a sinner.* Sin is you as you are.

In a strange way this is comforting, isn't it? Most people grow up with an image of God's angels as accountants keeping log books, peering down from heaven, muttering, "O-ho! Gotcha!" and marking down each error in thought, word, or deed. Now you are hearing from the Word of God that you were born to sin, that you are living out a destiny you could not escape. So you're tempted to say, "What, me worry? I couldn't help it." But this is really small comfort.

Face the Facts

You are still face-to-face with three facts you cannot escape.

1. You are born far from God, therefore you are not and cannot be perfect.
2. God holds you personally responsible.

3. Your destiny is dependent on the way you were born.

This is extremely hard to confront head on. This is who you truly are before God. You are a sinner. You are condemned. You *are* cursed. And there is no natural way out. You not only do not want to be this way, you do not want anyone else—including God—to know or believe you are this way.

Why not? Because if we admit we are imperfect, unrighteous sinners, we are in fact signing our own death warrant. Remember, "The soul who sins is the one who will die" (Ezekiel 18:4). To pick up *that* pen and sign *that* paper is suicidal.

Precisely because we cannot make that decision of death, we become enemies of God. We and God are on opposite sides, locked in mortal combat. There is no neutral territory. We are not Swiss. We are like a hungry dog chomping down on a scrap of meat snatched from the master's table. The master seeks to reclaim the stolen portion and to discipline his dog for breaking the rules of the table. But the dog snaps and growls fiercely, attacking its own master, all for the sake of the table scrap. The dog no longer is the master's dog; it has become his enemy.

That table scrap is your soul. It is your destiny. You broke the rules. Your table-scrap soul was God's portion from the beginning. But you wanted to hold it for yourself. And you are afraid to give it back. So you fight. For your life. Against the Master, your Maker and your Judge! It is a futile fight, snarl and snap as you will, for the custody of that dying scrap, your soul.

Oh, yes—confronting the finality of sin results in hostility, our hostility toward God. From that perspective we face God's anger. Diving to the depths of our nature before God will produce the most profound pain imaginable. Martin Luther called it "the most severe conflict within the heart." We rip the stone tablet from Moses and hurl it to the ground, shattering the first and foremost commandment—"You shall have no other gods before me." It is *this* God we battle. We want to shove and push everything possible between him and us.

I want you to face God now, as you are. Face your own teeth and fangs, for you are opposed to all that is God, love, right, and true. God is your mortal enemy, and he has the right to kill you. His Law has revealed it.

Face the anger, yours. Your destiny is not your own. Your will is chained and tied. As a dog on a leash in the yard circles the pole until the leash chokes it, so it is with our human will. Having inflicted the damage on ourselves, we bark and snap at the one who attached us to the leash. It is *God* who is holding you responsible for something you can never accomplish. And he knows it.

Face the fear, yours. Fear of the truth that gnaws. You are by nature, by birthright, a sinner. From God's point of view there is no good within you. Before God you are less than nothing. The coals of anger quickly become the ashes of fear before that realization. The hair-raising fear of a just punishment, of death, of eternal separation also takes up permanent residence just beneath your breastbone.

Just alongside your darkest fears there lurks terror, yours. For you cannot avoid your destiny. Like a man who takes a wrong step in a lumber mill and finds himself hurtling through a chute into the teeth of a buzz saw, you cannot avoid this encounter with God.

Face the anger, God's. Righteous anger for your failure to live up to the Law. Anger pure and clean and total. The wrath of God is now laid upon you.

For you to experience all of God's anger would destroy you here and now. To experience God's righteous anger will destroy you forever. When you face God as a sinner, you have also met yourself. What is your destiny?

 **Chapter 8**

Final Judgment

Whatever the law says, it says to those who are under the law, so that every mouth may be silenced and the whole world held accountable to God. Romans 3:19

The Righteous Judge

Headlines like those below scream and echo against the oak-panelled walls of the justice halls these days. We are a courtroom society, obsessed by the law. In New York City

---

GUILTY

INNOCENT

MURDERER FREE PENDING SENTENCE

TEEN GANG TRIAL BEGINS

BUS ACCIDENT FAMILIES SETTLE FOR $6M

---

alone, I'd guess we've got maybe a million lawyers. How many of you have been to court? You know all the legal lingo, whether you have done hard time or never faced anything worse than a nickel fine for an overdue library book. We are a law-and-order bunch. Those who are expert in technical terms call us a "litigious society." We know about bail, copping pleas, reduced sentences, unindicted co-conspirators, prosecutors, bailiffs (are they related to bail?), court stenographers click-click-clicking, deadlocked juries, perjury, depositions, torts and briefs, and the appellate division. There's a little Perry Mason in all of us.

So I find myself issuing you a subpoena. You are hereby enjoined to make appearance at none other than your trial, in a room apart, a hall of true and final justice. We are about to end the search for perfection. In court. Criminal division. Before the Judge. Facing sentencing. All that we have considered thus far has been a hearing of your case, #9,450,656,729 on the docket.

You have faced the living God. Not only is he the one who watches, he is also your judge. He is the Righteous One. When Jesus commanded you to be perfect, he placed you in relationship to your judge—"even as your Father which is in heaven is perfect." It is God's righteousness, his absolute perfection, that has brought you down, because you could not live up to it. God's Law revealed your terrible, terminal case of the shorts, for you have fallen short of the glory of God.

The prosecuting attorney in your case is gnarly, foul-smelling, stogie-waving, sneaky-snaky. You have been assigned the kind of prosecutor who seeks to dominate the proceedings with shouts, harangues, and grandstanding. All of his efforts are directed against you! Your primary accuser is the devil. He is truly the ancient, evil foe of humankind. He is a tireless lawyer on perpetual overtime, a denizen of the bowels of the system. We are told in Revelation 12:10 that Satan is "the accuser of our brothers, who accuses them before our God day and night."

The work of the devil in prosecution is not to convict you; the Law will do that. It is not to judge you; God is the Judge. No, the devil's deed is to drive you down a dark path to a precipice of despair from which there is no return, only a long plunge. "Go ahead, jump!" he whispers, having deceived you over and over to trust in your own ill-conceived instincts. "Go ahead, end it all," he prods, having flung your faults back in your teeth until you can only fall, helpless and hopeless. "Go ahead, there's nothing left," he argues, seeking to annihilate in your heart any movement toward trust in God's promises.

Beware this nefarious prosecutor. Beware the dragon! He breathes harsh fire, and such flames cannot be quenched by human strategy.

In a certain very real sense you stand before the Judge self-accused as well. You know what you have done, who you are by birth, by nature.

You cannot escape it. Your guilt is not only pronounced from outside of you, neither is it simply devil-induced. It lives inside you as well, which only makes it doubly painful.

Recently after our church suffered a series of break-ins, I thought I had a line on the identity of the thief. I went to hunt him down, rehearsing what I would tell him. As I strode in anger down the block on the hunt, I knew I had to say one important thing: "Unless you change your ways and bring back the goods, God is going to get you for this! Robbing a church! Have you no shame? God is gonna get you!"

Then I brought the guy to mind—an exconvict, homeless, on the run, friendless, penniless, with AIDS. I haven't found him yet, but I have had second thoughts. First off, as the Lord says, "It is mine to avenge; I will repay" (Romans 12:19). Mine is not to be judge and jury. Second, it isn't that God will get this guy; he has "got" himself. He has got nothing. He is going nowhere. And, finally, so much more is the pity and the reason for prayer.

Guilt before God comes from within and from without. I am not laying a guilt trip on you here, playing psychological games with you, trying to make you feel guilty. This is more than a matter of feelings. It is a matter of fact. Many of us spend our lives at sea on an ocean of guilt. It's as though we are in a rowboat, pulling for some far shore for all we're worth, yet time and time again being pushed back out and washed over by the waves on that guilt-edged ocean.

False guilt is no laughing matter. It cripples. It paralyzes. But authentic guilt covers you like a blanket before the living God. As the Bible says, even "all our righteous acts are like filthy rags" (Isaiah 64:6). Guilt is more than a condition; it is a verdict—and you know it is the only verdict.

So plea bargain. Try for an insanity defense. Go for a reduction. Turn over an accomplice. Anything.

All defenses of desperation have been tried. All the bargaining ploys and the special waivers have been utilized. Do you know how many of them work? That's right—not one.

Bear in mind that I am not speaking about a little mental game of pulpit-pounding to straighten you up. This goes deeper than that. A group of Lutherans from Queens and Brooklyn visit prisoners at a locally notorious penitentiary called Rikers Island. We've found ourselves welcomed by the chaplain there because we're unusual. We simply want to sit and talk with the prisoners, one on one or in small groups. The religious routine the inmates normally receive involves one or more spirited leaders waving pointy fingers, shouting at them in no uncertain terms, "You are on the road to hell, brothers!"—for an hour or so. Then follows a five-minute opportunity to raise hands in the air and change lives—a salvation moment. As the chaplain puts it, "When you say 'Raise your hands' to a prisoner, he will always obey. He's used to sticking them up. It would be dangerous not to. So salvation becomes a game for them."

There are no games here. Something has to give. This situation is terminal. You stand convicted.

The Ultimate Punishment

Guilty and convicted, you now await punishment. The punishment is death, and this death is eternal. What in the world does that mean? It means that the way you stand before God by birth—sinful and unclean, hostile and faithless, imperfect and unrighteous—is the way you will remain before God forever.

God's righteous anger will be all that you know of God.

That is eternal death. That is everlasting emptiness.

That is hell. That is the punishment.

It disturbs me no end just writing those words. There is a heavy harshness to them. They frighten. They paralyze. They trouble to the depths. As a pastor, I am no stranger to death. I have watched people die. I have had to tell relatives that their loved ones have just died. I have experienced death in my own family. It is hard enough to face death in a society dedicated to avoiding that discussion, without opening up the concept of eternal death.

I am a relatively emotional person. I receive and answer several three a.m. wake-up calls a week from myself. In the middle of the night I lie there in prayer and internal conversation wrestling through the problems of people I care for. My prayers are for peace, for an end to worry and conflict, about the loss of loved ones, and about the economic woes that drive folks over the brink. Do I have a burning desire to heap upon you or anyone else a load beyond the loads you already carry? No thanks. But this bothers me. Deeply.

Nor is it my desire to trivialize your consideration of existing before God's anger forever, making it an evening's parlor game. You have come down a hard road. You had to travel it. You have reached road's end. We stand here together. All of us mortals; the whole human race. This is the end of the search for human perfection.

It ends before the judgment seat of God. Listen to the verdict. Listen to *your* verdict: "GUILTY!" Receive the sentence: death of body and spirit— eternal death. You are perfectly unrighteous.

 **Chapter 9**

Bang the Gavel Slowly

Just as the result of one trespass was condemnation for all men, so also the result of one act of righteousness was justification that brings life for all men.
Romans 5:18

The New Verdict

Here you stand before the judgment seat, ready to throw yourself on the mercy of the court. "How can I get right with God?" you cry. "How can I be perfect? It is beyond me!" you wail bitterly. "I am lost. I am condemned. I have no hope!"

The gavel is raised. The judge prepares to pronounce the final sentence. His hand clasps the gavel. It slowly descends.

But now the oak-paneled door creaks open. Now another prisoner is led in, manacled. Your heart stops—THUMP! Your mind whirs and clangs like a lock clicking into place. Your eyes whisk back and forth, recording every moment in freeze frame. A focused shaft of sunlight, motes of dust swirling, beams off cuffed hands and shackled feet. It is the gleam of dead iron, but for you it is a glimmer of hope. With each slow shuffling step of this fresh victim, somehow you feel a breath, a breeze, a movement of hope within.

Now, even as your name is called to receive the final sentence, even as the gavel hangs poised in the air, this innocent victim steps forward in your place! He receives *your* verdict. He takes *your* punishment. He accepts *YOUR* condemnation. And the Judge, the Almighty Judge, the Just Judge, declares you to be innocent! This fresh face, those bound hands, those hobbled feet, that person has received your judgment.

The bailiff reads the new verdict. His dry, emotionless intonation strikes a joy so deep you cannot contain it. You hear, "In the matter of case #9,450,656,729, the *Law of God v. David H. Benke*, the defendant is hereby declared innocent, is acquitted and released from custody effective immediately."

Finally the gavel bangs. It reverberates. It pounds the wood beneath as if in slow motion, punctuating the final decree: "Case Dismissed."

Do you know what this means? You have been declared innocent—you are righteous! Before the throne of God you are declared perfect! There is no double jeopardy in this court. You cannot be accused again! "Who will bring any charge against those whom God has chosen?" the Apostle Paul questions boldly in Romans 8:33. "It is God who justifies [makes righteous]." And God has made you righteous.

This is the Great Exchange. The one who stands in your place is Christ Jesus. The great and just Judge is the heavenly Father, Jesus' heavenly Father—and yours. An exchange has taken place. A trade has been made. The only begotten Son of the Father stands in your place. He has taken upon himself what is yours: your sin and despair, hostility and death before the demands of God. Those have been lifted from you. They have been placed on Christ Jesus. And what is his has been placed on you. What is his is righteousness, innocence, perfection. These could not be yours—but they are now! You are perfectly right with God.

You are free to go. Go ahead! You are free! Your freedom, your destiny, your right-ness with God is a done deed. It has been accomplished. By Jesus. By his righteousness. By his death. By his sacrifice. By his perfection.

There is a weightlessness to this freedom, true freedom, permanent freedom. You begin to float. Like a helium-filled balloon, you rise. The burden of fear, as enormously heavy as the Twin Towers, is off your neck. Your head is lifted up.

The leaden load of guilt is purged from your conscience. You can breathe deep. Your lungs expand to exploding. The blood surges fresh. Your heart is lifted up.

The handcuffs of despair and uselessness locked in place by the old evil foe have been unlocked. Your arms are strong again for praise and for battle. Your hands are lifted up.

The shackles of punishment—the penalty of emptiness, the fearsome wrath of God forever, the darkness of eternal death—those great chains have been removed. Your feet take wings!

Can you imagine this scene? Can you sense the forces that would be unleashed in a courtroom if this actually happened—if a condemned criminal were declared innocent because someone else took his place? Whew! The flash of lights, the cameras, the shouts of disbelief, the wails of joy and gladness, the hugs and high fives—you can see all of it in an instant, can't you?

Can you imagine the forces that would be unleashed in a human heart set free, truly free?

Imagine no more! This is your trial! This is your case. This is not a scene from Perry Mason. This is your life at its deepest, most profound level. In Christ Jesus, who stood and stands in your place, you are right with God! You are perfectly right.

What Happened?

Sit down for a moment. Unwind in the Judge's chambers. He's asked you in. Calm down; let the adrenaline level drop; take stock of the impact of your liberated status; rub the redness out of your handcuffed wrists; rub the amazement from your puffy eyes; get a grip. What happened back there in court? Maybe *you* changed. Maybe the Judge took a look at you and decided, "Those beautiful eyes must be innocent."

Then again, maybe not. How could you change? You're the same worn out poor excuse you've always been. Still stubborn as the day is long. Still prone to error. Still not (let's use the *P* word one more time) perfect. Still (now the *G* word) guilty.

When I told my wife the courtroom story of Jesus taking our place, she, being a strong believer in law and order, immediately cried out, "No way! That criminal is guilty! How can he get off the hook? It's wrong! This happens all the time—the bad guys get released. Some lousy technicality and they walk scot-free. Some softhearted judge gives in and all the people victimized by the criminal get the short end of the stick. Even when God is the Judge, maybe *especially* if God is the Judge. I don't think it's fair."

I replied, "Uh, Judy, honey, I think you might want to change your mind. That criminal is *you*." She became more understanding, in a hurry. In fact, as I have described that courtroom scene through the years in homes and church classes, there are always strong voices of disapproval. Churchgoers tend to want to stick it to the bad guy same as anyone else. Until they find out *they* are the bad guys, that is.

This proves a simple point: We'll take all the mercy we can get when it's offered. Why? Because we know we need it! The leopard cannot change its spots. Nor can we humans change our wandering ways.

A Change in the Heart of the Judge

There is but one option. Something has happened to the Judge: He had a change of heart. And so it is. You have just arrived at a mysterious and wondrous spot. You are at the core of spiritual reality.

Now let me pose a really difficult question: How can humankind—you for instance, or me for instance—take it upon ourselves to examine the inner workings of the heart of God? By what right do we enter those chambers?

In those sacred chambers we are newly promised life, a fortress of hope that follows the declaration of innocence, and a righteousness that is perfect. How to undertake such a journey to the center of the universe—to the very heart of God?

We enter *by invitation* only. We shall never storm the doors of the heart of God. We enter *by divine grace* alone. We shall not gain admittance by the power of our reason. We enter through the gift of divine revelation, *through* the garment of *God's Word*. We cannot seek that inner chamber by will or work. The door to God's heart will be unlocked only *through faith*. Only by reading or hearing the Word of the Gospel are we converted, our hearts changed. Finally, we cannot come alone. Only *because of Christ* can we know the heart of the love of God.

The booming gavel set you free. It was music to your ears. Let us find out about the majestic symphony of God's eternal love.

 **Chapter 10**

The Righteous God Revealed for All

God was reconciling the world to himself in Christ, not counting men's sins against them. 2 Corinthians 5:19

Luther's Discovery

Martin Luther was a studious man. A digger. Like you and me, he wanted to know how to get right with God. He could find no peace, so he dug into the Bible. And the more he dug, the deeper a hole he dug for himself. He came up against passage after passage that spoke of God's righteousness, God's perfect perfection. Luther found no comfort in these words of God, because they only proved that God was perfect and Luther wasn't. Then one day while reading Romans 1:17 these words seemed to jump from the page: "For in the gospel a righteousness from God is revealed, a righteousness that is by faith from first to last, just as it is written: 'The righteous will live by faith.'" This passage transported Luther from deep in the hole to heaven. As he put it, "Here I realized that I had been truly reborn and had entered Paradise itself through open doors." He had uncovered the priceless treasure.

What happened to this German monk and professor 400+ years ago? It dawned like a sparkling sun over crystal waters in Luther's heart that there is a righteous perfection *in God* that produces life, not death, by faith. This Good News turned him upside down. He was never the same.

Your Discovery

The pounding of fresh blood in Luther's inner chambers echoes the boom of the judge's gavel that sets you free. You are alive. Your heart pulses with Paradise. You will never be the same.

How can this be? To face this Judge should produce only a withering, never-ending blast of anger. Yet you have received not a blast but an embrace. The watching God, the distant God, the just God is revealed as near, is disclosed in mercy and forgiveness, and shows justice in a declaration of innocence that sets you free. What kind of judge are we coming to know? What kind of justice have we received? Let me illustrate with an example of justice as it is normally served.

The Normal Process of Conviction

Recently I got nailed with a traffic violation for running a red light. Only I didn't really run the light. The traffic signal malfunctioned, skipping the amber and jumping from green to red. The traffic officer seemed to know the idiosyncrasy of this particular signal in advance, because he was stationed there at the corner just leafing through a forest of tickets.

So, armed with a passenger who'd seen the faulty light and with time-lapse photos of the signal (I am a very thorough guy when falsely accused), I go to court. There I'm sent to a room packed with violators. It turns out that every last violation from every last traffic violator in this room has been written by the same traffic cop at the same corner. Hundreds of us! And we are all H-O-T hot. We are ready to fight for justice. And ready to win.

The judge makes his entrance, is seated, and guess who gets called up first on the docket. Your favorite violator.

I'm ready.

"Sir," I begin, "I hate to be this blunt, but I didn't do it. I did not run a red light. The signal was faulty. I have brought with me both time-lapse photos indicating the absence of a functioning amber light and a witness who was in the car with me as I proceeded through the intersection."

The judge looks at me. Then he looks out at the crowd all leaning forward, all rooting me home, all hanging on my strong case, my powerful presentation, my clergy collar.

He says, "Let's hear what the officer has to say."

My opponent steps forward in full police regalia, even to the riding boots, and says, "This man entered the intersection after the light had turned red, and received a summons for so doing."

The judge turns to me and says, "Is that true?"

I reply, "Well, yes, but the light was faulty, and …"

"I think I have heard enough," the judge concludes. "You, sir," he turns to me, "are guilty, and will have to pay the fine plus court costs. You ran the light. Next case."

Imagine me, a grown man, with smoke coming from his ears.

Imagine me, considering the risk of contempt of court.

Imagine several hundred violators behind me listening carefully.

Imagine them now locating their wallets, preparing to pay up.

The judge realized that all cases would be lost if extra evidence were allowed in that court. All violators would have been excused. The system could not take it.

God's New Justice System—All Violations Removed

I am now telling you that the entire legal system that condemned you before God has been overridden in Christ Jesus. I am telling you that all violators have been excused, that all violations have been removed. I am telling you that Jesus was led into that courtroom for each and every case, from one to ten billion, from those next up on the docket to your grandchildren's great-grandchildren. I am telling you that the whole world, all humanity from Adam to Ziggy Zyzkowicz, from first to last, all who have been born and all who will be born, all of it has been brought into the embrace of the righteous Judge, the perfect Father, by and through Christ Jesus. The system could not take the Son of God.

"God was *reconciling* the *world* to himself in Christ, not counting men's sins against them," writes the apostle Paul in 2 Corinthians 5:19. In Romans 5:18 he states, "The result of one act of righteousness was justification that brings life for all men."

Do you understand what this means? Is there a dawn, a light beginning to shine in the tunnel of your soul? All the sin and all the guilt and all the punishment in all the lives of all the people who have ever and will ever walk the face of the globe have been set aside by God in Christ. *Justification* means simply that God's not holding your sins against you, that the slate has been wiped clean. For everybody. No sin, original or otherwise. No guilt. No punishment. All that stuff—the labyrinthine passages and corners of your mind— cleaned up! All gone, taken up by the reconciling activity of God in Christ. Our God is at heart a reconciling God. Enter the heart of the reconciling God!

What Is Reconciliation?

What is God up to? What does *reconciling* mean? If you're married and have been through the Saturday night fights on the home front from time to time, reconciling is not a strange concept to you. After breaking up, there is always (hopefully) a time for making up. Reconciling is making up. If you can't find a way to make up, the inevitable divorce is granted for not being able to make up. The legal beagles call it "irreconcilable differences."

Reconciling is the bringing back together of old buddies who got unbuddied, of friends who somewhere along the line became enemies. I overheard this conversation recently:

> *We always got along so well—for 40 years, I think. Then when her husband had the hernia operation, I ended up becoming her taxi service to the hospital for three weeks. Now, when I go in for my gall bladder, do you think my Eddie gets a ride to the hospital from them? Oh, no—no time now. I think they're just too cheap to cough up the gas money. Eddie ends up taking the bus for $3 and three hours. So we're not talking. I mean, the nerve of some people!*

Reconciling would mean helping old buddies to see past present hostilities to past decades of durable friendship.

Of course there are thousands of techniques for

making up. A dozen roses hand-delivered to the office, a personal note (not one of those prepackaged cards) that says "I'm sorry," a candlelit dinner, a heart-to-heart talk with admission of guilt and promises, promises, promises. When it comes to techniques for reconciliation, we've got 'em.

As a pastor my job in marital counseling is often to get hubby and wife talking to one another. Since I'm not the most advanced guy around, I possess very few tricks of the trade. One of my favorites is relatively simple. When Art and Irene (let's say) come into the office, looking very cloudy and cool, after prayer I suggest, "Who'd like to go first?"

Irene offers to begin. "I can't get this guy to talk to me, Pastor. He's so distant. What is his problem? Why won't he talk to me?"

Now I unveil my trick of the trade. "I don't know," I respond. "Why don't you ask him? There he is, sitting right there." I continue, "In fact, why don't you two just talk to each other about what's going on. I'll just listen in and say something if I feel the need."

Using this secret counseling trick, I often have sat and said nothing much more than a closing prayer and good-bye after two hours. Sometimes two people just need official permission to talk it through, to make up.

God's Reconciling Activity

When it comes to God's reconciling activity, it's a whole different ball game. The need is the same—to make up, to start over, to get things straightened out, to bring back together. But it's not as though there's a channel of communication there waiting to be tapped. It's not as though there's a willingness to sit down and talk things through. It's not as though a few tricks of the trade will patch things up with hugs and kisses.

In our case, sitting in one extremely large overstuffed chair facing backwards is the faithless partner: the whole world and everyone who has ever and will ever inhabit it, in "as is" condition. "As is" for us is hostile, stormy as a tornado, hot as a volcano, dead set against the will of God, unfaithful as outlaws. In fact, as we learned earlier, under the Law we have nothing to say. There are no excuses. We are in stony cold silence, for "every mouth may be silenced and the whole world held accountable to God" (Romans 3:19).

In the other chair is God, the offended partner, the aggrieved partner, who is also the counselor and divorce/family court judge. This is without question a case of "irreconcilable differences." Terminally irreconcilable. In this marriage, as the prophet Hosea writes, our love is "like the morning mist, like the early dew that disappears" (13:3). We have been unfaithful. We have said yes and done no. We have gone off with other partners down shady lanes. We have made claims. We have begged and pleaded on bended knee. And then we have broken all promises, over and over and over. There is no hope.

Except that God, on his own, while we and the whole world are yet in our sins and turned the other way, has made up with us. "I will heal their waywardness and love them freely," says the Lord in Hosea 14:4. In Christ, God has made up with you! And with the whole world. Forever. He has spun the overstuffed chair around and caused us and all the world to look into his face. It should be the face of wrath and doom. The divorce decree should be final. But when we behold him now, the Righteous One who reconciles, we behold grace and truth and endless love because we see Christ. And God sees us through Christ.

Off the Edge and onto Solid Ground

Understand, please, the *depth* and *reach* of this reconciling love of God. We live on edge. Today's make-up kisses form the basis for tomorrow's fight over their sincerity. Tomorrow's fight ends with hugs and hand holding. On the third day the hands are clenched as fists. And so on and so on. I'm not just describing a marital condition, but a condition of the world and the soul.

But in truth, God has reconciled you and the world to himself forever. He has taken us off the edge and onto solid ground. There is no return to former times. God is not like us. God does not harbor old wounds. God is not an ambiguous partner, blowing hot and cold. "God is for us," Paul wrote in Romans 8. God has reached beyond the yawning crevasse that separates us, and he has snatched us back off the edge to himself. He holds us tight. God *is* love. Christ is the proof, once and for all.

There is no simple way for me to describe the reconciling love of God. It's easy to describe God as an angry Judge. You can see the picture and feel the heat. But to describe the magnitude of God's love in bringing the whole cosmos back to himself, this is a mystery beyond recounting. The Bible word for that dynamic of love is *grace*. Grace is God's solid ground. Grace is so amazing that it lies completely outside of us and rests securely and solely in the heart of God. I could not and will not try to explain the grace of God beyond the way it is indicated, which is Christ Jesus.

The Movement of Fatherly Reconciliation

Luke 15 records a great story Jesus told about the reconciling God. Most likely you have heard it before. A man of means has two sons to cherish. The younger son comes up to dad one day and demands his share of the family wealth. He grabs it, takes off, and with all the gusto in him proceeds to blow it on wine, women, and song. Then, reduced to poverty in a far-off land, he finds himself amongst the pigs, a hand hired out to peddle pods to the porkers. There in the mud he comes to his senses. He decides to head back home. And then, on the road back home, the story goes, "while he was still a long way off, his father saw him and was filled with compassion for him; he ran to his son, threw his arms around him and kissed him." No hostilities, no reprimands, no "where's the dough, boy?" Just reconciling love running to meet the runaway child. Just the father's love, the father's kiss.

"He ran," the Bible says. A middle-aged man from the Middle East in the midday sun running, robes flapping, beard flying, arms flailing, dust puffing, lungs gasping, sweat pouring, tears streaming. "He ran." Where is the dignity in that description?

Ha! This *is* dignity described! The worth, the value of all human life, is contained in these words, "He ran." For the father's running love tracks the path of the son's cherished stature.

Imagine the fantastic flow of that love reaching down the corridors of time to 10 billion wandering children. Imagine God as a loving Father running in the hot sun, over and over and over again, to meet the children lost to sin and the grandiose delusions of the selfish soul. Imagine the fullness of the Father's presence as he comes closer, as he shouts, then throws his arms high in the air and embraces, and kisses *you!* This has happened!

At what cost? The Father's all-encompassing love for the lost cost him his only begotten Son. One Son for the billions, off in the wilds, headed down a road to nowhere, penniless and destitute. This is the exchange rate. This is the cost of divine love. One Son for the world. This then is reconciling love. This is grace. It begins and ends in the perfect heart of the Father.

My first memories of life on the planet revolve

around Dad's big hand holding my tiny one tight; Mom wiping away a tear after a tumble; Dad's shoulders with me perched on them, safe so high above the rough ground; Mom tucking me in with a goodnight kiss. All-embracing love in the family is our childhood fortress. The warmth of Dad and Mom's trust inside us is our reserve for the cold storms that will batter us. Those who have had to do without that parental trust face long odds in life.

How much more firm a fortress we possess in the loving arms of God! It is he who calls out, who seeks, who runs to meet us even after every dream of childhood has been shattered, even after we have run the other way, ridiculing his demands of love. He loves me yet! He loves you yet! He loves the world of his creation yet and always. In Christ, the Father has rebuilt the fortress and has set us high within its walls. Nothing—not sin, not evil, not death, not destruction—nothing can breach those walls. Such is the power of God's reconciling love for the world.

 **Chapter 11**

The Reach of Reconciliation

Christ died for sins once for all, the righteous for the unrighteous, to bring you to God. 1 Peter 3:18

Five Questions Answered

With the incredible energy of God's dynamic love fresh in your mind, let's address some questions buzzing through your brain right about now.

Who in the World?

First let's get at the full sweep of what God has done in Christ. He was reconciling to himself the world. The world includes everyone. Now that word *everyone* is kind of disturbing, this time in a new way. I indicated back a ways that everyone is under the curse of the Law of God. That bothered you because you were included, along with all the no-good losers of the earth. Now we're reading that God set the world right in Christ for everyone.

"Everyone who?" you ask.

"Everyone who ever lived," I reply, "or will live. Period."

Now you're back with the losers again. Some very ugly names and faces pop into your head—Hitler, Attila the Hun, mass murderers, the real worms of the world. The question is, has God been in Christ not counting the trespasses of these no-good bums? The answer is yes.

It's as though you were invited to a party at a fabulous mansion where heroes and people of prominent power mix and mingle. You get a sneak peek at the guest list, and all of your worst enemies, plus the inmates of the local jail, are listed— right there next to you.

If the system called the Law is to be overcome with any staying power, it must be overcome for all. Because, as you discovered earlier, everyone is under the curse of that Law. So on the other side of the verdict, everyone of the prisoners must be granted release. All the convicts, you along with Attila, must be declared innocent. The punishment attached to each and every conviction must be borne. As the Bible says so simply about Christ "He died for all" (2 Corinthians 5:15).

Take it one step further: If in Christ all convicted sinners, yourself included, have been granted release from the prison of the Law and its force field as well as from the punishment of God's anger, then have all benefited from that release? No, but that's an issue we will take up later. For now, believe what the Word of God says: "The result of one act of righteousness was justification that brings life for all men" (Romans 5:18). If this justification, or acquittal, were any less complete, you would be left in doubt, because there would have to be another system still in place weeding out the really bad guys from the so-so bad guys. Then Jesus' words about hatred being murder already accomplished in the heart might haunt you as you lay awake considering what you'd like to do to your boss or the guy who mugged you or the man who sold you the wrong flower bulbs. You would be left in your sin.

Be glad of heart and grateful that the trespasses of the *world* have been laid aside. For in that equation you have been acquitted.

How Can I Help?

A second question bubbling up inside you is, "If I have been granted this acquittal before God and if all the action took place 2,000 years ago when Jesus was on earth, what is there left for me to do?" Your perceptive question can be answered in one word: Nothing.

How then do you fit in? When it comes to getting right with God, you don't. When it comes to your becoming perfectly righteous, you cannot be involved.

"Not so fast," you retort. "I have to believe. That's what I do. 'The righteous will live by faith.'

This verdict, this change, this act of God in Christ must be believed *by me*."

Now I'm going to give you a short answer with a promise to get into detail down the line. The short answer is that the innocent verdict must rest securely in your heart of hearts. But if you had anything to do with placing it there, it will *not* rest securely. If you want some part in your acquittal, even "willing" it home, then you're back up against what you know to be the obvious imperfection of your will, the way you want all kinds of odd (and even unhealthy) things at various times. You will not be secure. You will not gain acquittal.

The fact that this acquittal has been accomplished in Christ stands in your great favor.

One Way or Many?

A third question for some of you might be, "Is this the only way? What about other ways of getting right with God? Other religions, meditation, New Age philosophy, Buddhism? You get right with God your way, and I'll do it my way. Won't that work?"

Two replies. First, the original system, the force field called the Law, applies to everyone, including those who, let's say, meditate as their way to reach God. Now no matter how good meditators feel after meditating, does it make them perfect? Do they show all signs of what we called "person sin?" Do all humans stand before the same Judge? Of course. All are in need of acquittal. That is the first point.

The second point is that there is just one way to that acquittal: "God was reconciling the world to himself in Christ" (2 Corinthians 5:19). That is the way. There is a great little word that says it all right here—the word *once*. Peter declared in his first letter that "Christ died for sins *once* for all." God's new deal is a one-time and one-time-only deal. There are no other alternatives—not in the past, the present, or the future.

Several months after Jesus' death and resurrection, a crippled beggar got up off the streets of Jerusalem and began jumping around. This incident caused all kinds of trouble for the Apostle Peter. It was he who had brought the cripple to his feet. Peter got nabbed by the authorities and taken into custody for inciting a disturbance. Cripples are not supposed to possess leaping ability. When asked in court how he had acquired restorative, healing power, Peter responded, "It is by the name of Jesus Christ of Nazareth, ... for there is no other name under heaven given to men by which we must be saved" (Acts 3:10,12). One name only, for one name is enough. God's action in Christ was a unique occurrence, once for all time. Christ is the way it is done.

Is God a Softy?

The fourth question might be, "What are you telling me about God? You said there is a change in the heart of God. Has the Judge gone soft? Is that what all of this has been about?"

Keep one thing in mind. The Bible says you

have been *declared* innocent. Your trespasses have not been tallied against you. It does not say that you *are* innocent. Apart from Christ your verdict stands. Put another way, the Judge has not gone soft on crime. The Judge hates sin. He hates evil. He is not responsible for, but in fact stands totally opposed to the flaws his Law reveals. The perfect righteousness of the Judge means that he remains perfect and righteous and just. What you are just beginning to learn is that this very perfection, this very righteousness, *applies to you.*

Is This Just a Game?

"But then," you continue, "are you describing merely some kind of game with me as a pawn, or what? The way it feels is that God drives me and everybody else to our combined 12 billion knees inside his system just so he can tell us to get up off our 12 billion creaking knee bones because we have been set free by a third party named Jesus. Is this fair?"

This question reminds me of certain bad murder mysteries. In these non-Agatha Christie type mysteries, when the plot gets so thick it becomes sludge, when it's so tangled and messy no one could unravel who done it, the author resorts to a surprise character, a never-before-seen Mr. Smith, and he becomes the culprit. This bothers avid mystery readers because they feel they were led along a path with no end. A game was played on them.

Has God been playing games with you? Indeed not! Your condition by birth is desperate. That's no game. That's the truth. You stand by nature facing the everlasting anger of God. You cannot solve this condition. That's the bottom line.

There is no internal solution. Just terror before anger. Just life at the edge of the cliff. Only an outside source can bring perfect righteousness. That source is Christ. And if all twelve billion plus knees are not unlocked by that new and precious resource, there is still terror in the air.

It is not a game. The Son of Righteousness was immersed in sin. Paul tells us, "God made him who had no sin to be sin for us" (2 Corinthians 5:21). God's total dedication to making right that which is wrong led to the very real temptation, the very real suffering, and the very real death of Jesus, God's only begotten and perfect Son. God was reconciling the world to himself "in Christ," the ultimately real gift of death for life and life unto life.

The question period is over. I have just described God's new deal. It is not called the Law, but the Gospel. It is not deduced, but revealed. It is not for the few, but for the whole world. It is absolutely at God's initiative. And it absolutely depends on the very personal work of Jesus Christ.

 **Chapter 12**

Christ Jesus:
Perfectly Righteous
Friend of Sinners

*The Son of Man came eating and drink-
ing, and they say, "Here is a glutton
and a drunkard, a friend of tax collectors and 'sinners.'" Matthew 11:19*

Who Is This Jesus?

I t is time to meet Christ Jesus. It is time to
meet the one brought forward to take your
place, your punishment before the Judge. It is time
to test all the claims made about the way life is,
both under God's Law and under the power of
God's reconciling righteousness.

Maybe you have felt the weight and movement
of this book driving you toward this encounter
with Christ. Trust those feelings! That, I can tell
you, has been my purpose.

There is no other way to understand God except in and through Jesus Christ. There is no other way to understand human destiny—my destiny, your destiny—except in and through Jesus Christ. There is no filter through which to funnel reality except through the judgment and mercy of God revealed in Jesus Christ.

The biblical record of God's dealings with humankind reaches its sharpest, most intimate focus in Christ. This is the prime purpose of the Bible—to reveal Christ and, thereby, to create faith in your heart. It all comes to a head in the person and work of Jesus, who was called the Messiah, Anointed One, the Christ. It is he. There is no other. God makes an exclusive claim on the world, on you, in his only begotten Son, Jesus. This I believe. Now who is this Jesus? What I wish you to know is that Jesus Christ is the perfectly righteous friend of sinners. He is a friend to me.

But how can you be sure? Today you can hunt down almost any version of Jesus you could dream up. Jesus comes in all colors, with all accents, in all kinds and types of garb, short hair or long hair, blond hair or brown.

Of course, you cannot peek backward 2,000 years in time. But for the past several hundred years, dedicated scholars have tried their best to sift through what was available before the invention of photography—writings, documents, tombstones, and shrouds—in what has been called "the quest for the historical Jesus."

What have they come up with? Mostly this quest has been a paring process, like what you do to an eight-ounce carrot. By the time the peeling is done, you're left with a sliver of orange root, an hors d'oeuvre. Most of the words and many of the acts of Jesus have been sliced from the Bible in this "scholarly" paring process. The resulting hors d'oeuvre editions give us Jesus as a great moral teacher, or Jesus as the liberator of the poor, or Jesus who died as a revolutionary in revolutionary times, or Jesus about whom many wonderful ancient authors invented fascinating stories for reasons of their own, or Jesus the peacemaker, or Jesus the righteous man whom God later adopted as his own Son. I'm not kidding. All these editions of Jesus are floating around in very respectable circles. But Jesus is not an hors d'oeuvre; he won't be cut to bits.

While this "quest" has been an impossible dream developing into a nightmare, the reaction to it has not been spectacularly focused either. Highly "spiritualized," weird, and bloated editions of Jesus have been lifted up to counteract the "he was only a human" version. "Put in your mind the image of Jesus as you see him, then make him smaller and smaller until you can walk him down inside your body where he can grasp the cancer cells in your colon and remove them," one faith healer goads you on. What? Is this a science fiction movie—*Innerspace Goes Holy?* Where did this apparition come from? Christ cannot be manipulated like some inflatable pawn on a magical chessboard.

Our Perfect Friend

Instead of these highly manipulatable versions, meet Jesus, the perfectly righteous friend of sinners. This description fits the Jesus of the New Testament.

I had trouble putting those two concepts together—"perfectly righteous" and "friend of sinners." The first concept seems to put Christ at a distance. It paralyzes me. If you were to introduce me to someone at a party by saying, "Dave, I'd like you to meet my friend Bud, perfectly righteous in every way," I would most likely begin beating a hasty retreat. I would be tempted to treat that person as an alien life form, as a cold fish, as too remote for me to ever truly approach. I'd be constantly worried about offending. Does he have x-ray vision? Can he see my secret thoughts? Does he know that even though I'm a registered Democrat I sometimes vote Republican?"

On the other hand, if you were to introduce me to someone by saying, "Dave, I'd like you to meet my friend Bud, who is and always has been a friend of sinners," I would respond, "Then you must be a friend of mine, Bud. Glad to meetcha." I would hunt down the nearest McDonald's and share a burger and fries with that person and seek to get to know him better. We might have some laughs—maybe lots.

Meet Jesus, the perfectly righteous friend of sinners. You need not fear his righteousness, his perfection. In fact, appreciate and enjoy those qualities. They are there for you. In fact, it is his righteousness lived to the full on your account that most makes him your friend!

Read His Record

Consider the way Jesus lived. Even as he calls sinners to repentance, he lambasts those who claim to be the good guys, righteous law-abiders. With a startling whiz bang, he shouts fire and brimstone at them left and right. And the feeling is mutual. The folks who look for all the world like the good guys, the upstanding citizens, the ranks with the right stuff, spend their time trying to trick Jesus, to put one over on him.

But then, with no advance warning, Jesus visits the much-hated Roman stooge tax collectors, women of ill repute, outcasts, the feeble, and the frail. He sits down at the table with *sinners.* These meals are "on the record." They are included in the four books called the gospels. There is something of great significance in these meals with sinners. At the table a unique encounter takes place. And who is it that these normal everyday people encounter? The Billy Joes and Mary Ellens and Buds of the day—the sinners—who is it that they meet?

They meet a Jesus who is different from them. This is understood immediately. He is not a sinner. He is an altogether different sort of person, with a capital *P.* John the Baptist, Zacchaeus, Peter, the

Roman centurion, all of these and many more meet the righteous Jesus.

And what do they say? With Peter, they confess, "We believe and know that you are the Holy One of God" (John 6:69). They immediately experience his holiness. He is not like them. He fulfills the Law; he does not break it. He is actively obedient to God's higher purpose. He is connected in a profound way to the Father. He is righteous. He is holy.

It is impossible for those who meet him to pretend they are anything other than what they are: sinners. This is why those who claimed to be righteous couldn't stand the sight of him. He would not let them escape their true condition.

And yet he sits down at the table with sinners! He, of his own free will, becomes an equal with them and rips apart the "don't cross this line" barrier that the Law puts up between true perfection and imperfection, between righteousness and unrighteousness, between the blessed and the cursed.

In fact, he claims to have the right to forgive the sinners' imperfections. "Take heart, son," he tells his friend, the soon-to-be-former paralytic, "your sins are forgiven" (Matthew 9:2). Thus are broken all the barriers between God and humankind in the Person of Jesus.

Meet This Jesus

Meet this Jesus. He is the perfectly righteous

friend of sinners. He was actively obedient to the Law of God each day of his earthly existence. He is not some emanation from the highest heaven bearing lightning bolts. The apostle John spoke of him: "The Word became flesh and made his dwelling among us ... full of grace and truth" (John 1:14). In the words of Paul, "When the time had fully come, God sent his Son, born of a woman, born under law, to redeem those under law" (Galatians 4:4); "In Christ all the fullness of the Deity lives in bodily form" (Colossians 2:9). This makes him unique in all history. Christ is both Son of God and Son of Man in one full and complete person. Jesus, the Holy One of God, was born under and behind the force field called the Law, and there made friends with sinners. That, friends, is good news!

Would Jesus be your friend, then? Would Jesus sit down with you? Would he sit down with me? I know a man who sits and talks with Jesus every day. His name is William Lee. A devout Christian originally from the island of Jamaica, Mr. Lee is an elder at our church. And he is a man of prayer. Most times when he begins a prayer, Mr. Lee does so in this way: "O Lord Jesus, we come to thee today speaking as friend to friend ... " Jesus is his friend.

"How do you know Jesus is your friend, Mr. Lee?" I asked him one day. "Because he listens to me," William replied. "He sits with me every morning from four o'clock when I wake until 6:30 when

I leave for my work. I tell him everything. He knows me to be a sinner; but even so, he loves me."

"So," I countered, "you tell your friend Jesus all these things every day for two or three hours? That's a long time! What are you praying for? Who is on your mind?"

"Why, Pastor," he responded, knocking me over with love, "I am praying for *you*." Mr. Lee is a dear friend of mine. More important, Mr. Lee has told his friend about me!

I gave some thought to what might happen if Jesus were to appear suddenly in my kitchen, and the two of us were to share a burger and a brew. After all, I fit snugly into the sinner category. What might happen, after we tossed through the ball scores and the sports trivia, is that a moment of truth would arrive. Just as it occurred to the disciples at Emmaus, a moment of profound recognition would arrive. Recognition of the Holy One of God. Recognition of his concern for me.

I would seek from Jesus, as did his friends who followed him long ago, the power to change. The power to repent, to confess, and to start anew.

With a friend named Jesus, there would be no need for secrets, for hidden agendas. There would be no point. His holiness overcomes all such tricks of the human trade. Total disclosure would be the only option across the table.

In that disclosure I would seek to know forgiveness from my friend. I would seek to know firm purpose for my life. So I would seek from him love and the strength to love in return.

In point of fact, these kitchen conversations with Jesus are a daily occurrence for me. I know this for sure, because God has created faith in me though his Word of grace, the Gospel. Therefore, I need my friend, and our conversations are always good. I sing to him sometimes, songs of love. Songs that are prayers, like this one:

Jesus, priceless treasure,
Source of purest pleasure,
Truest friend to me;
Long my heart was burning,
And my soul was yearning,
Lord with you to be!
Yours I am, O spotless Lamb;
Nothing I'll allow to hide you,
Nothing ask beside you!

Follow Your Friend

Yes, Jesus is your friend and mine—sinners, all of us. Righteous, he alone. Yet he has befriended us. Follow your friend now. Through faith, receive his forgiveness offered to all—to you—in his Word. Follow him to the place where his friendship takes him. You see, in the personal friendship of Jesus, you have been thrust into the most titanic clash in the history of the universe. The irresistible force of God's reconciling love is meeting the immovable object; the status of the world under the Law. The two cannot coexist. But Jesus is in the middle. He perfectly fulfills the Law, and yet sits down at table with sinners, with you and me, and makes sinners his equals. Through his Word, he announces their forgiveness, their acquittal before the judgment seat.

The Law continues to demand its payback, its retribution, its death sentence to those who do not obey it in full. You stand under this sentence, yet Jesus has sat down with you. He has dared to cross the line. He has the power to forgive sins against the Law whose demands you cannot fulfill, even as he has fulfilled them.

You know where his friendship must take him, then, don't you? He himself has told you: "Greater love has no one than this, that he lay down his life for his friends" (John 15:13).

 **Chapter 13**

The Cross Marks the Center

For the message of the cross is foolishness to those who are perishing, but to us who are being saved it is the power of God. 1 Corinthians 1:18

The message of the cross ... is the power of God." These simple words are the supreme assault on the human spirit and at the same time the supreme hope of the human heart. How can the power of the living God be revealed and released through a message fixed upon death? How can perfect righteousness wind up on a cross? Why is this particular death anything other than another human tragedy? What makes this death the very "power of God"—so different from all others? How can this message actually accomplish the thing it describes?

At the Foot of the Cross

The grand finale of Jesus, whom you know as the perfectly righteous friend of sinners, takes place not in a banquet hall but in a garbage dump; not where champagne toasts punctuate the celebrations, but where vinegar on a sponge dulls the pain; not on a podium with awards and speeches for a job well done, but on a bare wood cross with a crown of thorns and hurled curses. Our search for perfection is stopped—dead—at the foot of the cross.

We and all others could not face the Judge and stand. We are not perfect and never could or will be. The Law has condemned us. What followed that condemnation was this: Jesus was brought to stand in our place. Where? On the cross.

Didn't I tell you that he lived a perfectly righteous life, that he was in deed and in truth the Holy One of God? Where did his righteousness lead him? To the cross.

Didn't I tell you that he was a friend of sinners, that he was your friend? Where did that friendship take him? To the cross.

Jesus hung on the cross at the center of the turning world. Meet him there at the foot of the cross.

The Cross: Symbol and Reality

The world is filled with crosses these days. The cross is one of the few religious symbols the ad execs haven't stolen to sell cars or laundry detergent. Maybe that's because the cross just isn't very distinctive any more. And maybe, just maybe, with the billions of crosses found on everything from granite headstones to diamond necklaces, we have lost sight of what the cross of Christ means.

Of course, even then, 2,000 years ago, his was just one cross among many. Crucifixion was the capital punishment of choice for the Roman Empire. But just one cross counted—the cross of Christ.

The Power of the Cross

How exactly is this cross the *power* of God? Consider it with me.

1. Jesus, in his own words, "lay down his life for his friends." He died freely, on purpose. He died for us, his friends, and took our guilt upon himself. You and I cannot carry an ounce of our own weight before God, much less anyone else's. Jesus literally took the moral, legal, sinful weight of the world upon himself. Talk about the strength of Atlas—the cross requires far more power!

2. The power to bear the cross came from God, for what Jesus did was the will of the Father. Jesus, says Peter, "entrusted himself to him who judges justly" (1 Peter 2:23). Catch the power in that sentence! Jesus entrusted himself to his Father, the just Judge, who must and did administer the just punishment, which was death. God the Judge administered the punishment exactly by the book, according to the law of retribution. He exacted

punishment against his own beloved Son. The power to take away punishment was taken upon Jesus. And it is the will of God.

3. The curse was removed from the world. That incredible dangling sword, sharp and pointed right at you, swings and slashes, knifing the air—but it cuts Jesus, who hung on the cross. Our common curse, the flaming sword of death flashing back and forth, was removed by Christ on the cross. He caught the burning sword and held it in his own seared flesh. Thus a power far brighter was unleashed.

4. There is no more condemnation. Trespasses are not imputed. The billing department calculator does not spin out the unlucky numbers of your sins until the tape with your name on it clacks to a conclusion. The Law, God's handwritten and heartwritten deal, a deal designed to stop the mouths of all, is itself stopped cold. Why? Because *all* the trespasses of *all* the people for *all* time have been put on the bill of the one on the cross. Paul says it best: "He forgave us all our sins, having canceled the written code, with its regulations, ... he took it away, nailing it to the cross" (Colossians 2:13–14). The powers and authorities and everyone and everything that clings to that written code were hoisted up there, too, and disarmed.

5. All that forgiveness, all that righteousness becomes yours when God uses his power in the Word to turn your heart to faith, to turn you to trust in his grace, which is offered in the Gospel.

Power in Weakness

On the cross everything was turned inside out. The universe was topsy-turvy. Jesus hung on a cross, absolutely powerless, weak, forlorn, homeless, forgotten, dying. Yet there the system of the world was beaten. There all the power players who thrive on exacting punishment and big-bucks rewards from that system were held up to ridicule. They don't matter anymore. There the Holy One of God, who knew no sin, became sin for us.

The strength in the cross's weakness is in its reach. On the cross Christ reached through the system of the Law to you and me at our weakest, most vulnerable, most mortal spot. Then he took the Law unto himself. In the taking of my sin, and yours, and ours, unto himself, there became a strength beyond measure, which is now found only in the weakness of the cross!

Wisdom in Foolishness

The cross is foolishness. It does not, it cannot, it will not make logical, straight-line sense.

I heard a very earnest young man recently trying to pull some teenagers into the Christian camp. He hopped up on stage and started off with a bang.

"You kids are *stupid!*"

The kids I was sitting next to kind of jump. They flinched. Inside, they said "Ouch!" They began to look for an exit, to dream up excuses to get away from this abuse.

I thought, Lovely! Way to win 'em over!

The young man continued by just laying into

these ordinary kids, who were messing up and trying hard not to, just like 94 percent of the developing persons between 12 and 80 do. He labeled
all the stuff they like as "dumb, worthless, useless."
He ranted on that they're going to have to pay for
it. Then after about a half hour he turned the table.

"Get smart! Get with Christ!"

During all this, I was thinking, "Here's a guy
who has it exactly 180 degrees wrong. Exactly
inside out."

Kids, as I know them, are incredibly smart—
what we call here in Fun City "street smart." They
know what's expected of them and how to get it.
They watch MTV. They know what to wear, how
to shop, how to spend, how to go for it. And they
follow that yellow brick road with all the wisdom
and courage they can muster. They're not stupid.
And at some point they realize, even in those formative teen years, with all the hyped up marketing
forces united to get them to consume, and with all
those hormones in high gear, that they are being
sold a bill of goods. They are being handed a bundle of fast and easy solutions that really are no
solution. The wisdom of the world doesn't work!

Now they sit on our church doorstep, looking
for true wisdom, for real and lasting and honest
solutions. And what do we have to offer?

What we have to offer is true foolishness,
which is the cross of Christ. To follow and call
"Lord" a perfect person who ended up dead—
where is the wisdom? To believe in a God who

gave up his only begotten Son for a world absolutely and totally committed to a course of rebellion and disaster—does this sound like the kind of choice wise people make? It doesn't take a rocket scientist or a street-smart hustler to walk away from a loser. We hate losers. They're stupid.

The cross of Christ is, for all the world, a loser's message. Wrapped in pain and a dead giveaway, it is a present nobody wants. It is a promise failed. No amount of sweet-smelling ointments can mask the odor of death.

But *this* foolishness, *this* weakness, *this* cross, *this* death is the power of God, the wisdom of God, the strength of God, and the source of life with God. It is, in the words of St. John, sheer glory. For by this foolishness humankind is set free. God has played the fool, running after you in the midday sun, giving up his only begotten Son unto death to save your sorry neck. It is wild. It does not make common sense.

The foolishness of the cross of Christ can hit you like a guy who rushes around a corner with an armful of boxes and crashes into you. Boxes flying, bodies tangled—all you can do is pick yourself up. And all of a sudden on your way home, you stop and double up in laughter, thinking of that guy and his packages flying all over the intersection. And when you think of the cross of Christ, after you meditate solemnly, after you pick yourself up off the ground, and after you cry out from the pain, don't be surprised to find yourself grinning a lopsided grin from ear to ear, all of a sudden the happiest creature on earth. Smile for us now; grin that foolish grin. I think you just realized it—you're a fool for Christ!

Preaching the Cross

If you merely nod and take the cross of Christ for granted, as though that is the way things have to be, *wake up!*

In the cross of Christ the world is turned upside down. Death brings life. There is light in the midst of darkness, glory in the midst of total despair. The force of evil and the power of sin are not beaten by a big-bang God bopping the bad guys with bolts of lightning. The force of evil and the power of sin are not beaten by armies of angels or billions of prayer warriors or raptured believers exiting the planet by reading the tea-leaf signs of the times. The force of evil and the power of sin are not beaten by well-educated, progressive philosophers, politicians, and industrialists who promise to rid the world of hunger, clean up the environment, and still take a healthy profit by the year 2020. And even if angels and industrialists somehow banded together and put a pollution-free, renewable-energy automobile in every garage (a project I favor for both angels and industrialists), you would not be perfectly right with God, would you? The force of evil and the power of sin would still propel you down beneath the smoking system that flings its curses.

No, the force of evil and the power of sin were brought to nothing, absolutely nothing in the death of Christ on the cross. As T. S. Eliot put it, "not with a bang but a whimper." And in the silence of the last expiring breath of the Holy One of God, it was finished.

 **Chapter 14**

Where, O Death, Is Your Sting?

If Christ has not been raised, your faith is futile; you are still in your sins.
1 Corinthians 15:17

Where, O death, is your victory?
Where, O death, is your sting?
1 Corinthians 15:55

Ray

In January 1981, the phone rang at five in the morning—a bad sign. It was my mom. "Dad had a heart attack. He died in the middle of the night." I sat in bed and shook like an aspen leaf for a good hour, unable to cry, but out of control. I was in no way prepared for that news. Who is? My dad had given me, his eldest son, an heirloom pocket watch only the summer before. Did he know somehow his time was short?

He spent his last evening on earth with my mom on an evangelism call, asking an elderly couple, "If you died tonight, do you know where you would spend eternity?" Then he told them about heaven. Did he expect to be used as an object lesson?

He woke in the middle of the night with an upset stomach. He went and sat down in his favorite chair, burped, sighed, suffered a massive heart attack, and died within five minutes. Ray Benke was 71.

Where, O death, is your victory?
Where, O death, is your sting?

Dick and Etta

Etta and Dick Lieberman lived across the street from Judy and me at 63 Norwood Avenue. They were like our grandparents. Married for over 50 years, they knew every tiny aspect of each other's behavior, and yet they were still in love. Etta couldn't give up smoking, but Dick hated it; so she, a 75-year-old woman, would hide a pack in the basement and sneak down a couple times a day for a few puffs. Dick would wait till there was an audience and Etta was just within earshot, then he'd bellow out, "Oh, yeah, I know what she's up to. She never darkened the basement doorstep before, but now she's down there four, five times a day, killing herself with those weeds." And Etta, in the next room, would mutter, "Ah, Dickie dear, we've all got to go sometime. Just leave me in peace."

To get his goat, all Etta had to do was produce a dime. "And who is this, dear? Whose face is on this dime?" Dick would roar, "The Great American Destroyer, Franklin Delano Roosevelt, that's who! I contend that bum ruined this country." And he would ramble off on a tangent for an hour or two, while Etta interrupted every now and then, egging him on, "Oh, not again. Don't go through that story again."

I was with both of them as they died. Both had but one request of me. "Pastor, can we read John 3:16?"

And so we recited the words together in hospital rooms harshly lit, death's observatories—"For God so loved the world, that he gave his only begotten Son, that whosoever believeth in him should not perish, but have everlasting life."

Where, O death, is your victory?
Where, O death, is your sting?

George

George Colon is six years old going on 117. Too young by far, he's seen it all. A zapping bundle of electrostatic energy more massive in mischief than Mad Max, George Colon is my godchild. His foster mother, Clara, brought him to be baptized. Judy and I were proud to be chosen as godparents.

On the day of George's Baptism in September 1990, I addressed the congregation with these words: "Tomorrow, thousands of babies born addicted to crack cocaine will enter the school system of this city. These children will be hard to manage, difficult to control, energetic beyond containment, unfocused, angry, emotional. That they are here at all is an answer to prayer, for these children were born with death in their veins. Death they had no share in. Death that controlled them while they were yet within the womb."

I paused to let this sink in, then went on: "I would like to introduce you now to one such child. You have already met him at the baptismal font. His name is George Colon. Love him with the love of the Lord, for he is now part of your family.

"See him at six days, bald and not so beautiful, in painful withdrawal from cocaine addiction. See him at two years, left to ride on the subway beneath the streets of New York for 12 hours by his mother, who forgot him from within her unholy habit. See him as he is.

"But look a bit deeper. For he is a mirror of you. We have all been born with death in our veins. We were born rebellious, on the brink of extinction, as far from God as night is from day. And yet, by the power of the Gospel, our God has claimed us—and George—for his own. Eternally. In victory."

Where, O death, is your victory?
Where, O death, is your sting?

Power beyond Death

Confronting death is like facing the lash of a whip. It cuts and bites and stains and digs. The pain lingers and spreads. I have taken such a lacing from death in my family and congregation. My dad's death as well as George Colon's life keep me in mind of my own mortality. Surely your own confrontations with death have left you similarly scarred.

How can the apostle Paul taunt these mortal blows? How can he throw them off, lift them up to the breeze, claim the sting is gone?

There must be a power that is stronger than death. Otherwise we would be left without hope. The death of Jesus opened the universe to the power of God, for God countered the system and its curse with the death of his own Son. "The sting of death," claims Paul, "is sin, and the power of sin is the law" (1 Corinthians 15:56). The cross cut off death's sting, because Christ endured the mortal lash in our place.

But if the cross is the final, ultimate stop in the search for perfection, we are left without hope. Christ in his death took our sins away, fulfilling the law of retribution: an eye for an eye, a tooth for a tooth, one life for all lives. But if in fact he died and nothing more, if a good man hung on a cross and gave up the ghost, then the grave would still claim final victory. "If Christ has not been raised, your faith is futile; you are still in your sins."

But thanks be to God, the grave could not, did

not make final claim upon the Holy One. "He is not here;" said the angel, "He has risen!" (Luke 24:6). This was the ultimate grave robbery. Not that someone stole the body of Jesus. Too many witnesses say otherwise. The gospels are full of the reports. Paul says that over 5,000 saw Christ alive. But on that Sunday morning, the grave was robbed of *its* victory. Forever!

Ultimate Victory

Death is not the final victory; the resurrection of Christ is. It is his final and ultimate word concerning life and death. When you face God in the Risen Christ, you face life, you face righteousness, you face perfection that will never end. This tyrant death, which cut an endless, permanent swath through all classes and races and families, has been beaten in Christ Jesus. Death rules no more. The throne belongs to Christ!

Some folks don't seem all that thrilled about the resurrection of Christ. They play it down by focusing on the community: the disciples and other followers. Such folks talk of a so-called "spiritual" resurrection of Jesus, of him as an disembodied ghost who "appeared" mostly in the minds of the beholders, rattled as they were by the fast pace of events in far slower times. What is important, then, to these folks is not whether Christ was truly raised, physically, from the dead, but whether you believe it.

To this I would simply reply, "You can't have

one without the other." Eight days after the resurrection, Jesus came and stood among his friends. He said to the disciple Thomas, "Put your finger here; see my hands. Reach out your hand and put it into my side" (John 20:27). He was telling Thomas quite precisely, "I am not a ghost."

You and I, of course, were not there. And yet I am asking you to believe. Just as Jesus declared to Thomas, "Blessed are those who have not seen and yet have believed." Perfect righteousness involves belief. But it involves belief in Jesus, who lived, suffered, died, and was raised. This is the Gospel, the absolutely Good News in full.

As Paul says, "He was delivered over to death for our sins and was raised to life for our justification" (Romans 4:25). The Gospel would remain the Law—in an ever louder voice—without the resurrection of Christ. But in his life, fresh and new and forever, the system has been conquered.

Me, I am overjoyed by that news. Ray, Etta, Dick, George, and I have gotten us a victory through the Gospel. You cannot walk the slow walk to the cemetery behind the coffin of your father without mourning. You cannot witness the soul-numbing abuse heaped on child after child even from within the womb due to the death-dealing demon of drugs without feeling pain and grief and hot anger. But there is a power that overwhelms even grief. There is a Strong Warrior who knocks aside even the devils that, as Martin Luther sang, "the world should fill, all eager to devour us." Christ is our power over death. Christ is our Strong Warrior. In the words of the hymn, he is our "Sure Defense." He is our only defense. In his resurrection, life holds, life endures, God's life prevails.

Believe it! It is for you!

 **Chapter 15**

For You and Me: Perspectives on Saving Faith

For it is by grace you have been saved, through faith—and this not from yourselves, it is the gift of God—not by works, so that no one can boast. Ephesians 2:8–9

It is time to talk about you. There is no more important topic in the world. Surprised at that? Well, I mean it. I have been including you all along, of course. When we were talking about the fact that everyone has a conscience, yours was included. When we spoke of the force field called the Law of God, you were among those hemmed in. When we went before the Judge, your case was called. When the Judge let Jesus stand in to take human verdicts, you were declared innocent. So you shouldn't feel left out.

Now we need to get even more personal. We turn our attention to you and your response to the Good News of God's grace in Jesus Christ. Humans have devised many ways to respond to God's gift of grace. The response we will be honing in on is called "faith." It is *your* faith that counts. Your personal faith. As our friend Martin Luther realized from the words of Paul, "In the Gospel a righteousness from God is revealed, a righteousness that is by faith from first to last."

New Perspectives

When we start talking about you, about your interior design, about your faith, I don't want your head to turn. I don't want you to get all wrapped up in yourself. That would be fatal. In fact, it would show a real lack of concern on my part, because if I led you down an interior path to the place where God and you communicate, where grace meets faith, and you got totally confused by the messy mass of signals in there, you would be left in torment. Hung up, so to speak. Or if we took that journey within and you somehow got the impression *you* were able to take care of things between you and God by virtue of the strength of your own inner convictions, I would have introduced you to a false god—one with your initials.

I am most concerned that saving faith be yours forever. And that means examining what that very difficult word *faith* means for you as you stand before the living God. Let me suggest that you open yourself up to a different perspective from the one you normally take when thinking about yourself or your belief. Turn things inside out.

That kind of change in perspective was forced on a half dozen of us on a narrow street in Paris one summer night. Our tour bus made a sharp turn down a dimly lit one-lane road. Suddenly the driver jammed on the brakes with a screech. Forty of us on board craned our necks to see the problem, which was immediately apparent. A red car was parked right out in the middle of the road. There was no room to pass.

The bus driver, Helmut, began muttering furiously in a language with lots of deep guttural sounds—a bad sign. Then he called out sharply, "I need six men. Now!"

I jumped up and ran to stand behind the bus, thinking to help him back it up to the wide safety of the main street.

Helmut was having none of it. "No back up. Nein!"

"So what do you want us to do?" I asked, my perspective limited to what I saw as the only natural course of action, namely reverse.

"Ve moof car!" he dictated.

"Move the car?" I laughed. "You gotta be kidding, Helmut. We can't! That thing weighs a ton. We don't have any equipment or anything."

"Ve moof car now!" he repeated.

A new imperative, a dynamic new perspective,

was revealed to us by someone far bigger and stronger.

Pick up the car and move it off the road! And do you know what? The seven of us picked up that car and moved it.

Helmut took the front end, and the six of us red-blooded American guys handled the rear end like champs. We eased on down the road like heroes, with a whole new perspective on big-city motoring and problem-solving. Don't back up the bus; move the car!

Now let's try that change in perspective when it comes to the journey within, to the level of faith.

"Think about yourself," your mom encourages.

"Consider yourself," the philosophers urge.

"Get in touch with your innermost self," the pop psychologists egg you on.

"Get a grip on yourself," your frustrated friends dig.

What all these well-meaning helpers want you to do is to back the bus down inside. This is what is called *conventional* wisdom: The deeper you go, the more you will find and the better you will feel. If you know yourself, you will find comfort and strength. Put her in reverse, and inhale those diesel fumes.

I am saying that we've got to move that pesky car out of the way to proceed. We have got to get *you* out of the way! I am saying, the deeper you go, the *less* you will find. In fact, you're not going to find anything useful down in there. So you need to look somewhere else—on the outside. And there will be Christ—for you. You will not just *feel* better. You are going to *be* better. In fact, you'll be the best! Let me elucidate (I like that word) by stating five perspectives on saving faith.

Faith, Not Deeds

"We maintain," says Paul, "that a man is justified by faith apart from observing the law" (Romans 3:28). Perfect righteousness has been our aim. Perspective 1 is that you arrive at that righteousness by faith and not by deeds. This one is easy. You know what the Law of God does to you: it accuses. It does not let you off the hook. So, any system that pretends to set you free by obedience to the rule book is doomed to fail. You can't lug enough greenbacks or major accomplishments before the altar of God to get you right with him. Count all that "good" stuff, even the time you visited Aunt Luella in the hospital every day for two long months, and your grand total is the big goose egg.

In order to receive "this righteousness from God through faith in Jesus Christ," Paul decided to dump all that other stuff. It was as worthless to him as it is to you. I "count them but *dung*," he put it quite elegantly (Philippians 3:8 KJV). Reminds me of a certain *día de mojón,* a doggy-doo day I once lived through.

As nice as you may be, it doesn't do you any good when it comes to getting right with God. Neither niceness nor neatness counts. It's time for a perspective change. Do you want righteousness? Then do not begin with the things you do. Try another starting point.

Faith's Object: The Gospel

Begin instead with the object of faith. Perspective 2 is that the object of faith is always and only the Gospel. Let us not get distracted. God's reconciling, graceful love shown in the gift of Christ, who lived, died, and was raised for us, is the starting point in front of all other starting points when it comes to faith. It is something accomplished "out there" in the world at a specific time and place in history.

Saving faith isn't about your belief that the sun will come up tomorrow. It's not about your belief that your feelings are sacred. It's not about your belief that you are worth saving. It's not about your belief that short people try harder or that rich people get richer. So keep your faith perspective on the Gospel, God's gift of grace in Jesus Christ. But, you ask, how?

Faith According to God's Power

"Your faith," said Paul, "[does] not rest on men's wisdom, but on God's power" (1 Corinthians 2:5). The power of God is made perfect in the cross of Christ. In fact, when Paul dropped all gimmicks from his preaching and stuck to the cross of Christ, only then his preaching proceeded "with a demonstration of the Spirit's power" (1 Corinthians 2:4). Faith was created in the hearts of hearers by the

Spirit of God through the Word of God. This is the ground of faith.

Perspective 3 tells you that, since saving faith cannot be worked out by you, it is worked out by God.

Is this clear? Faith is not something you do. Faith is not the best thing you can do for yourself. Faith itself is a gift of God through the Gospel.

This should be of the greatest comfort to you. I am telling you that the bus is already at the terminal—and you weren't even driving! The car blocking your way is gone and you didn't touch it! All obstacles have been removed from the road to righteousness. You are there. Faith is God's free gift.

This is the only way it could ever be, to be honest. Faith just cannot be a matter of your *trying* to believe, laying awake late into the night telling yourself, "Come on now, get with it, you old sausage; have faith, have faith, believe, believe." You could try and try until you popped a blood vessel, but you could never blow down the wall of hostility between you and God. It doesn't matter if you try harder.

But not to worry. Saving faith is God's work in you! If faith depends on your acceptance of the new terms, then get ready for a long winter, because you are bound to reject those terms on general principles or lack thereof.

"But," you ask, "how does this happen?" You keep asking that.

Faith Resides in You

Finally, we are ready to discuss the "in you" aspect of faith. It took a long time to get to you, and I hope you are happy about that. More of God, less of you. You have not been asked to accept faith as a good all-over feeling or a try-harder attitude or a sense of drawing closer to God. Saving faith is God drawing close to you through his Word of grace.

Perspective 4 turns it back around—for saving faith is in your heart, your mind, and your will.

You cry, "My heart, my mind, my will—I thought we would never get there. I need that faith inside of me, and you've been holding back. Tell me what it means that faith is my heart, my will, my mind believing in Christ." Okay, I will.

We are now inside that person you lovingly call you. Saving faith is the reliance of the heart on the promises of grace, the knowledge in the intellect of what God has done, and the confidence in the will to receive the forgiveness offered in the promises. Home is where the heart is, and by faith God has made his home in your heart. He has gotten there through his Word, whether spoken, read, or meditated on.

Take immediate notice. I am not leading you down the garden path to rejoice in your faith, am I? Rejoice instead in the promises of God.

Notice something else. I am not making a case for locating faith in your emotions or in your mind or in your will. You are you—a combination of all of the above.

Your intellect tells you the facts of the Gospel, what God has done. But mere facts are not faith. Faith informs and fulfills those facts with a very personal content. They are facts accomplished for you.

Faith is not just a good all-over feeling about Jesus. If faith were only a feeling, then when you felt bad, you would be fresh out of faith. You would feel forced to "put on a happy face" no matter what. Still and all, the warm desire of faith is real.

Faith cannot be limited to the confidence you have in God's promises, but your will is definitely made confident in faith.

Saving faith, to be saving for you, must be in you. It must be your personal saving faith. That is why the Bible locates it in your heart, your soul, your will, your mind.

"But," you ask, so well trained by now, "isn't it true that the Bible says 'I know that nothing good lives in me'? Isn't faith a 'good' thing inside me?"

You have asked a very tough question. It is of the greatest importance to millions and millions of Christians around the world who have a soft spot in their hearts for their own faith. I want to speak with tremendous love and concern for all who take pride in the birth and growth of their faith, in the day they "turned to Jesus," or "accepted Christ" into their heart. Many folks have been led to have faith in their faith—which is a false and dangerous hope. But if that's not the way faith works, how does it?

Faith Works from Outside In

Perspective 5 tells it all. Saving faith works from *outside in.*

Charles S. Dutton was the leading actor in a Pulitzer prize-winning play entitled "The Piano Lesson." During an interview on the TV show "60 Minutes," it was revealed that Dutton came to Broadway the hard way. He had been in prison. He had killed a man. In discussing the changes he had undergone, Dutton said, "In jail I got to thinking how small, how tiny, how insignificant my life really is. How it is just a dot on the horizon in the overall scheme of things." From that changed perspective, Dutton began to realize in reverse what a great gift life is—and to feel remorse for murder. Starting from a dot on the horizon, he came to see the beauty of life.

This perspective reminds me of the words of Psalm 90: "Lord, you have been our dwelling place throughout all generations. ... For a thousand years in your sight are like a day that has just gone by, or like a watch in the night." Our lives are indeed like dots on the horizon, like grains of sand on the seashore from God's eternal perspective.

When you get "outside of yourself" like Charles Dutton did, as we all can and must, something happens. What is "you" doesn't expand.

Instead, you shrink. Down to a dot on the horizon. In that shrinking there is an element of self-judgment, of self-accusation. You realize how little you matter in the overall scheme of things. You and your 70 or 80 years and your golf clubs and your car and your memories are a dot, a grain, a blade of grass.

Put that perspective on yourself before the Judge, and you begin to realize that God's Law brings you to nothing. God's Law reduces you to a cinder before his anger. This is the essence of terror before anger. This is the end of you. This is the beginning of Christ.

Saving Faith: Christ Covers You

At that dot, the righteousness of Christ covers you. There the cross of Christ reaches you. There saving faith is created by God. There you, empty of all sauce and spunk, all hope and pride, grasp the truth: Christ's death is your death. Christ's life is your life.

There by the power of God you grasp, you hold, you seize, you cling to Christ and to the very mercy of God. This is the way faith receives the promises of God. Saving faith is not some kind of psychological change. It could not be, or faith would depend on something in you, the receiver, and not the Giver. Faith is at its core "out there" where the dot named you is covered by mercy, where a Word of God in Christ is spoken to you, a sinner. This is saving faith from outside in.

Saving Faith against the Grain

Saving faith from the outside in goes absolutely against the grain of all the therapeutic cures on the market today. How many millions of copies of how many thousands of books haven't told you to "get in touch with yourself?" And how many Christians and non-Christians haven't seized on those books as a source of help?

Gerald May, a respected doctor who deals with addictive personalities, requests readers to experience the "heart," the core of being. "The problem," he writes, "is that this heart sense is so spacious." The next step, he says, is to experience this spaciousness, which is "not quite oneself nor quite God" in order to find security, confidence, and spiritual growth. Many religious leaders and self-help promoters are selling the same line but put it neither so eloquently nor so clearly as Dr. May.

Yet I am telling you that saving faith demands exactly the opposite structure of that reality. Saving faith in Christ is the strongest spiritual force human beings experience. It works not outward from a vast and strong inward experience, but inward from a dot on the horizon outside of you. There is no security in you; no confidence that begins in you; and no spiritual growth that can proceed from the core of your being. Your security, your confidence, and your spiritual birth and growth must be given to you.

And they have been—in Christ, through the Word, the Gospel of your forgiveness.

He Is All in All

Now by God's grace it becomes possible to understand with the insight of faith this simple sentence: You are not your own; you were bought with a price. Now those mysterious words of Jesus have meaning: "Whoever wants to save his life will lose it" (Luke 9:25). And now, most of all, saving faith becomes certain faith. For saving faith depends on the God revealed in the Gospel alone, and not on you. Your heart, your will, your mind, none of which could stand up to the scrutiny of the Judge, have now been filled, by faith, with Christ. He is all in all. Thank God: he did it all!

 **Chapter 16**

Christ Is All My Righteousness: The Assurance of Salvation

God made him who had no sin to be sin for us so that in him we might become the righteousness of God. 2 Corinthians 5:21

Christ Is Our All in All

I s Christ your all in all? He is mine. I know it. And I am not ashamed to say so. I am certain of his righteousness!

We all have watershed moments in life. Looking back on them, we ponder, "There, right at that point, I finally had to take a stand. I had to make my choice." It could be a personal problem and a final admission that you couldn't handle it. It could be a job change. It could be you happen upon a robbery in progress and have to decide whether to duck for cover or jump in with both feet. It could be the death of a loved one. But you are called in those moments to take a stand.

Centuries ago, Martin Luther, an ordained priest threatened with excommunication from the church of Rome for teaching the truth as he knew it about God's perfect righteousness in Christ, got up before the Holy Roman Emperor and declared, "Here I stand! I can do no other." He received excommunication papers in the mail shortly thereafter that are still in effect. But the powerful message of God's love for the world revealed in Jesus was released. That stubbornly courageous declaration was a watershed moment.

I had one of those moments in a cemetery. Chandra Thackurdeen's mother, Aswatie, had died of a heart attack. I knew Aswatie, originally form the South American country of Guyana, to be a Christian. We had prayed together at her bedside. So when Chandra asked if I would perform the funeral service and preside over the burial, I immediately said yes.

When we drove up the hill in the Bronx cemetery, I discovered all of sudden that the family had deep roots in Hinduism. A pandit, a Hindu priest, was there waiting for us with family and friends.

This was going to be a new experience for me. There is no seminary training course entitled "Hindu-Lutheran Funeral Resources." Normally, I wouldn't even let myself get into such a bind, but there we all were. I couldn't very well run off the pandit and (for all I knew) maybe half the family. Besides, I wanted them all, including the pandit, to hear the promises of God in Christ. So I took the funeral director and the pandit aside and asked, "How do you men think we should proceed?"

"Father," the funeral director said to me, with a very earnest note of discomfort in his voice, "I think it's all up to you." (In New York, no matter your wedding ring, your wife, and your 12 children by your side, if you are wearing a clergy collar, you are going to be called "Father.")

"Well, my son," I replied, laying a hand on my newest child's shoulder, "as long as you leave it up to me, I believe that the pandit and I should both take a turn. It's only fair."

This was exactly what the funeral director least wanted to hear. He took my hand from his shoulder, guided me off to one side and whispered, "Listen, Father, who knows what might happen here? It's *your* funeral. You came with the hearse. Let him watch."

"No, no," I whispered back. "You've got it wrong—twice. First of all, it's not *my* funeral. Not yet, anyway. Second, we can't just ignore this man. I think we need to respect everyone who has come here. We each take a turn."

"Well, just keep it quick," he muttered. "It's a long way back to Brooklyn."

Now the pandit and I began negotiations, as the family and several hundred onlookers of East

Indian derivation waited on the hill with the coffin. In truth, we made a few false starts and propositions. After all, on what page is this order of service found?

Finally I made a decision. "Look," I said. "Why don't you go first, and I'll finish." This was agreeable. And so commenced Aswatie Thackurdeen's funeral service.

The pandit made extended remarks from his faith experience, commenting on Aswatie's goodness and the cycles of life through many reincarnations. Then followed a ceremony in which rose petals, saffron, incense, and other items we carried were strewn around the coffin in a circle as symbols of peace and rest, as aspects of the cycle of life. All were invited to participate by circumnavigating the coffin with the pandit, dropping rice and rose petals. But no one moved.

Now came a moment of truth. Politeness, yes. Respect, yes. Growth in understanding, definitely. But from way down deep inside me there came welling up this simple, all-inclusive, exclusive thought: "Jesus died ... Jesus lives ... Jesus is Lord!"

That thought, that belief, that sentence could not be dislodged from my being in that moment. *Christ was all in all in me.* The pandit finished, and bowed with respect for me to begin.

In the soft rain of spring in that cemetery I reached down very deliberately, took a handful of dirt, lifted it in front of me, and declared, "Life has a beginning and an end. 'For dust thou art, and unto dust shalt thou return.' 'The sting of death is sin, and the power of sin is the law.' Aswatie is dead. Her body will return to dust.

"But Christ has also died on her behalf. She has confessed her faith in him. And because he lives, she too shall rise to life in him. There is only one true God, and I say 'Thanks be to God! He gives us the victory through our Lord Jesus Christ.' All who believe these words, please take the dust of the ground into your hand and place it on the coffin as I do."

Slowly the family and friends stepped forward to the grave, each and every one, forming a long and solemn line. Stooping to grasp the handful of dirt that describes us all, lifting it to signify their faith in the God who has gained victory over death in Christ, and laying it on the coffin in tribute to the everlasting life-giver, they took their stand, as did I. Christ was all in all for me.

(I'm thankful that, under these rare circumstances, no one thought that Hinduism and Christianity have equal footing. Lest someone think that, I'd never give prior agreement to such a joint service.)

Although that was my personal experience, I sincerely hope you have been taking all of this personally. I sincerely hope you possess the assurance of your salvation.

Our search for perfection is over. You have been made righteous by grace through faith on account of Christ. That simple sentence is the Gospel for you. You have a new suit of clothes. All the old, worn-out garb—the Nehru jacket, the bell-bottom jeans, the suit with the shiny spot on the seat of the pants—throw all of it out the window. The protective garments you wore like a cloak or overcoat before God, the "looking good" garments you wore like a tuxedo or a ballroom gown before God, they are now "like filthy rags." You are wearing Christ. You are perfect, because he is perfect.

Once upon a recent time I got into a big mess with your and my favorite tax collection agency, the Internal Revenue Service. I was serving on the Board of Trustees of a local hospital that had financial problems and declared Chapter 11 bankruptcy. Following bad advice, it also failed to pay to the IRS employee withholding taxes.

After a period of time I received a letter from the IRS declaring that I, as a trustee, owed the USA, with interest and penalties compounded every minute on the minute, $1,400,000 (give or take a few bucks). My life, at least in the fortune division, came to a screeching halt.

The clock was running, and as far as I was concerned, it was "another day older, and deeper in debt." I was told that this type of penalization could last from six to twenty years, with extensions up to and including my last will and testament, at the government's discretion. It could be a sentence *beyond* death!

Finally, after seven years, my ace lawyer and others got the case to court. After some months, I received a phone call.

"The verdict is coming in today," said Adeline Malone, my lawyer.

Have you ever seen a grown man bite a phone cord, begging the phone to ring? Have you ever waited seven years beyond your endurance level?

Finally, RRRRIIIIIINNNNNNNGGGG! I picked it right up. "What? What is it?" I shouted. "Tell me true."

"We won!" the shout came back. "It's over—we won!" I sat down on the floor and wept and thanked God, a millionaire in reverse, finally back to even.

But do you know something? It never really sank in until I got a letter from the IRS several months later. "There has been an adjustment in your account," stated the anonymous author. "On March 15 you have a BALANCE DUE of $1,400,000. As of March 16 you have a CREDIT of $1,902.37."

I threw the letter up in the air, made copies, and laminated the original. I began laughing and couldn't stop. I felt lighter than air. My friends and I floated over to Pop's Ice Cream Parlor in Woodhaven. We had us a feast—root beer floats on the house!

Then I went out and purchased, on my own, with no help, a brand new Banlon golf shirt, which

I believe to be the finest single item of apparel available for sale. I was free. My debt had been canceled. I had the receipt to prove it. And I had a brand new shirt to show it off—my garment of righteousness.

There is a level to faith that I would call "the assurance level." There is an experience of the mercy of God that is more real than paid-up tax receipts and Banlon shirts. More real because it is deeper than death. It is far beyond the reach even of the IRS. It is as deep as the heart of the living God.

Paul said, "We also rejoice in God through our Lord Jesus Christ, through whom we have now received reconciliation" (Romans 5:11). He is the receipt—paid in full! He is the cost, received in our heart through faith. You can be certain of your salvation! You can be absolutely certain of your righteousness because God himself gave it to you through his Word in all its forms.

Lights-On Faith

Faith, when it receives such news, is active. It leaps, it jumps, it runs like the prodigal son toward the father. Faith is no cold calculation, like an accountant who totals up the numbers, closes the books, and goes home for the night in neutral, thinking, "After all, they're just numbers." Faith, brought into being by the Holy Spirit outside of me, at the dot on the horizon, becomes an embrace in my spirit. It is an embrace that never ends, with a Jesus who is eternally my merciful friend.

This is the way I look at my life with God: I knew my need and it was met in Christ. I'll stick with him. It's sort of like what happened with my neighbor, Dotty. We had anticrime lights installed in our backyard. Dotty began to fuss. "I do not see the need for those beeeaamms shining in *my* yard," she would complain. "Right in the window in the middle of the night! Turn the doggoned things off, please."

Then a little crime wave washed through the block, touching all homes by night *except* those with lights in the yard. "Say," Dotty approached me one day, "you know one of your bulbs is out on those anticrime lights. Better get it fixed."

"Excuse me?" I asked. "You want these lights to burn?"

"Well of course," she responded, kind of sharply, too. "I'm buying my own, but they won't be installed 'til next week. You really ought to look after yours more carefully."

When the need grew great, the lights went on.

So has our need been met in Christ. We act in faith, like a woman turning on the switch of her newly-purchased bulbs. Christ is the lamp that brightly burns. God says, "Light this lamp. Put on this righteousness. Wear my Son like a robe. Take your stand. Say it out loud. Speak what is in your heart."

Faith brought to the heart responds to the graceful invitation to take it.

Faith and Amazing Grace

Recently I was recounting the story of Sir John Newton to our parishioners. Many of their ancestors were either brought forcibly by or bought and sold into the service of the British Empire. Several hundred years ago, Newton was the captain of a slave-trading vessel. According to his notes, one day when a storm arose at sea, instead of his usual oaths and curses he uttered, "Lord, have mercy!" The Lord had mercy. The storm abated. Newton journeyed on.

In fact, a new journey had begun that day for Newton, a journey of faith. Eventually, he would lend the strength of his stories concerning the evils of the slave trade to the work of a man named Wilberforce. Slavery was brought to an end in Britain.

You all know John Newton, though, or at least his work. For it is he who wrote the hymn "Amazing Grace." Imagine that hymn now as written by a man who stood on the bridge of a boat carrying human cargo for trade. Imagine anew what God can do.

People were moved when they heard this story of saving faith as I recounted it. One man, though, asked urgently to see me privately.

"I need to know how you came to tell this story today," he looked me in the eye, when we sat to talk.

"Saw it on TV," I replied. "I have the tape. You can take it home if you'd like."

"No, no," he continued, leaning forward. "I just have to tell you that God saved *my* life this week when I said those same words: 'Lord, have mercy.'"

"What?" my eyes grew wide. "How did it happen?"

"Well, Pastor," he said, speaking slowly and carefully, "I have been having a terrible time at home. Nothing is going right. It's all falling apart. So late Sunday night, I decided to end it all. I got in the car, drove to an intersection, waited for a truck, and when I could see a big one bearing down on me, I gunned the accelerator."

"Good grief!" I interrupted. "You shouldn't even be here!"

"Pastor," he grasped my hand, "you don't even know the half of it. Just as that truck was about to make contact, I thought of the Lord, and my kids, and my wife. And the only thing that came into my mind was 'Lord, have mercy!'"

"Then—BANG—the car was absolutely totalled … and I walked away without a scratch! What does it mean? Why am I still here?"

We talked then, and prayed plenty, too, about his past and his future and his family. But at the heart of the matter was one thing only: not this man's problems, not his broken desire to live a good life, not his cry in the moment of utmost need, but only the mercy of God.

This man was not driving perfectly. He was out of control, lost, and in despair. But even then the

Lord had mercy. The righteousness of Christ was his all in all.

You do not have to be the captain of a slave-trading vessel; you do not have to get hit by a semi-trailer truck; you do not need to fall millions of dollars in debt; you do not need a face-off with a Hindu holy man in order to understand the mercy of God. The mercy of God is "new every morning" (Lamentations 3:23). In his Word of the Gospel, God's mercy is available for all of us in any condition. The point is, the mercy of God in Jesus Christ is available for your condition. The death and resurrection of Jesus has brought perfect righteousness, innocence, and blessedness to you and all believers. Of this you can be sure.

 **Chapter 17**

How to Live the Perfect Life: In Christ

Since we have been justified through faith, we have peace with God through our Lord Jesus Christ ... and we rejoice in the hope of the glory of God. Romans 5:1–2

S till Perfect after All These Years." I had to laugh at the guy I saw wearing the designer T-shirt with that graphic. Bald, with thick glasses, teeth missing, and a stomach twice the size of his chest, he was a walking advertisement for *im*perfection. Yet I'm sure he wore the shirt just for that reason. He wanted to draw a chuckle from passersby. Because perfection is simply beyond the grasp of us mere mortals.

I have made some extravagant claims in this book, based upon the Word of God. I am claiming that you are, in fact, perfectly righteous before the judgment seat of God in Christ Jesus. I am claiming that this is absolutely certain because God accomplished it for you and gives it to you through his Word. Your designer T-shirt could read "Still Perfect after All These Years"—as long as you added the words "In Christ."

Now I am going to tell you how to live the perfect life. It shouldn't really be all that difficult. You are, after all, perfectly righteous. Try on that T-shirt. You are perfect. It's enough to make you blush, isn't it? I mean, you—perfect. Me—perfect. As they say, "Who'da thunk it?" Never fear; the perfect life is yours!

What does this mean? No more slice on your golf swing? All bills prepaid? No more colds or runny noses? All dreams come true? No more secret sins? No more problems? Nothing but blue skies at your honeymoon hacienda?

Now, now; let's be real. Perfection in Christ means far, far more than you may have ever expected.

Perfect Peace

First, perfection in Christ means peace. Real peace. Perfect peace. The peace "which transcends all understanding" (Philippians 4:7). Ninety-nine percent of all the people who come to see me with problems state simply, "I am just not at peace. I'm depressed/agitated/angry/upset/down-in-the-dumps. I can't find any real peace."

The perfect life in Christ brings perfect peace. Listen to the apostle Paul: "Therefore, since we have been justified through faith, we have peace with God through our Lord Jesus Christ, through whom we have gained access by faith into this grace in which we now stand."

Where does that peace rest? Perfect peace is peace *with God.* The hostilities are over. Warfare, hatred, rebellion, tugging and pulling and boxing with the God you know to be your judge—all of it is over. You have been brought back together with God forever in Christ through faith, and nothing can take that away from you. It is true. This peace transcends—goes beyond—all *human* understanding, because it begins in the heart of God! You can go to bed every night secure in the knowledge that God is "for you." You need not doubt or fear that this condition is going to change, either. For faith, which does not depend on you, rocking and rolling through life, has received the Rock named Christ who has come to you.

If real peace only occurred when all your problems were gone or your enemies dead and buried, you would never have real peace, would you? Yet you can have a perfect life even when things go wrong! How? Because perfect peace is yours from "Good Morning, America" to "The Late, Late Show." It is peace with God.

Do you think an eternal outbreak of peace between you and God is going to affect the rest of your life? I hope so. The end of the struggle between you and God is the beginning of the peace process in all other relationships. It is a perfect start to your perfect life.

Perfect Honesty

Next, perfection in Christ brings honesty. You can't be honest in life until you have faced the truth straight on. In addition, you can't be honest until fear has been removed. In addition, you can't be honest until your self-interest has been covered and you are secure. The way it works down here on planet earth, in order for coverups, dishonesty, and question-ducking to disappear from human life, there has to be nothing to gain by being dishonest. There can be no need to cover up.

This is your situation. There is no need to cover up, because your sin has been laid bare on the cross of Christ. Naked and without excuse, you have faced the living God, and Christ Jesus has covered you. You have been excused. There is nothing to gain by lying before God, because everything has been gained already in the death and resurrection of Christ. Now we can talk about honesty in daily life with God.

First of all, it is now possible to be honest about your shortcomings. It is possible to acknowledge sin, weakness, fault, and flaw. Living faith not only allows but encourages, even demands, that you do so. Living faith, working from outside in, continues to monitor and accuse you while seeking refuge in Christ. Living faith is not cover-up faith, but ultimately honest faith.

Living faith knows you as a perfectly righteous saint of God in Christ, and yet as one who continues to sin. That is your honest condition on planet earth. You are a saint and yet a sinner. Living faith encourages you to convict sin inside of you so as to obtain the mercy of Christ, who was righteous for you.

"I don't know where to begin," Mary sobbed. She had come to me in turmoil. "I've been to therapists; I've read books; I've prayed. I even went to a priest. But nothing makes this go away."

"What is it?" I asked. "What hurts that bad?"

"Five years ago I had an abortion," she confessed, looking to me for reaction. "I didn't love the guy, and it just happened, and I made the decision to have the abortion. But it just won't go away! Was I right?"

"What do you think?" I responded.

"No—I know it was wrong. Everybody else tells me I was not wrong to do it, but I *know* it was wrong. What do you think?"

"I think your conscience is just telling you what you already know from the Bible is true—that it is wrong to take a life."

She looked at me in deep pain and anguish. "You are the first person I've found who said that, who told me the truth, who told me what God says. What can I do? What can I do?"

"Look," I responded. "I think I know why

you've come to me. What is torturing you way down deep is not just you and your baby. It's also between you and God, isn't it?"

She nodded.

"The pain you're feeling isn't just the loss of that life; it's also that you're facing God and you don't find love. You feel abandoned."

She began to weep. "Yes! I can't even turn to God with this. It's too much. God can't forgive me!"

"Listen," I plunged on, "Listen carefully. You are sorry for this—I know that. Aren't you?"

Mary nodded yes, head down.

"Do you believe in Jesus?"

"Oh, yes!" she responded immediately. "He's all I have!"

"Then I can tell you that God can forgive you; God does forgive you; God has forgiven you in Jesus. Let it go. Let it go."

And she did.

Mary came in honesty to receive honesty from God and his Word. She received mercy and pardon.

An Honesty That Excludes Phony Perfectionism

This honesty is a very powerful truth. Many Christians are forced to play games because of what I would call "phony perfectionism." Many Christians have been convinced that real Christians don't sin. If they do, so they reason, then they are no longer Christians. They no longer have faith.

Some would even say that a true Christian cannot get sick.

A woman came to me some years back with that theory. She was insistent and would tell anyone else who was sick that the cause of even a headache was lack of faith. So I monitored her for a few months. Finally she came down with a cold.

I confronted her, "Norma, you're not coughing, are you? I thought you couldn't catch a cold anymore, with that perfect faith."

"No, no," she wheezed, "I don't have a cold. It's just the wind."

A few days later, she was even worse. I went to visit her.

"Quite a wind, Norma," I began.

"No, I *do* have a cold," she sobbed. "It must be my faith. It must be something I did wrong. I'm not a perfect Christian. It's my fault."

"You have got that right on the runny nose," I responded, teasing her. Then we began to talk. We talked about being a saint and a sinner at the same time. Honesty had won out.

Phony perfectionism is kind of frightening, don't you think? It is also very senseless and damaging to self and others. The damage is done because people are encouraged to have faith in faith, not in the perfect righteousness of Christ. Healthy, saving faith demands a daily and thorough self-examination, admitting weakness and clinging to the mercy and pardon offered in the Perfect One, Christ.

Perfect Love

I don't mean to say that your life has to be a miserable mess where you beat your breast and hug the ground, weak-kneed and wimpy. No, the perfect righteousness of Christ is the power source for our third benefit, a perfect life of love. Once again, the apostle Paul says, "The life I live in the body, I live by faith in the Son of God, who loved me and gave himself for me" (Galatians 2:20). Saving faith *forms* my life. Saving faith gives me the power to live the life of Christ.

Martin Luther said, "This [Christ's] life is in the heart by faith where Christ reigns with his Holy Spirit, who now sees, hears, speaks, does, and suffers all things in that person, although the flesh does resist." I can walk in newness of life, knowing it's my gimpy legs taking the steps, but Christ directing where those steps take me.

"Direction" is one of the prayer requests made most often before the altar of my church. When you've been lost and you "get found," the next question is "Where am I going?" Directions are needed: guidelines, a road map. Many churches more or less order Christians at this point to pick up a two-ton weight filled with dos and don'ts: don't drink, don't smoke, don't wear pants if you're a woman, don't wear makeup, do attend church meetings five nights a week, do give to the poor, do, don't, do, don't … Life becomes a type of locally explained, detailed street map drawn from the big map called the Bible. This map can confuse and bring that "Uh-oh, I think I'm lost again" feeling.

The Good News isn't a set of rules for living. The Good News is a perfectly righteous person named Jesus, who, under God's direction, died and was raised to life for me and now lives in me through the Gospel.

He offers a much simpler set of directions for life, directions called "love." Addressing his Christian friends, Paul said, "Love is the fulfillment of the law" (Romans 13:10). Faith acts in love because love has been received. The motivation is as pure as pure can be, because it is not a human motivation. It is not forced. The perfect righteousness of Christ provides the motivation.

Peter spoke for the 12 disciples and for all believers when he said, "We believe and know that you are the Holy One of God" (John 6:69). That Holy One in you is actively loving and caring for others. Martin Luther put it well: "Christ fulfilled the Law perfectly, for he loved God with all his heart, and with all his soul, and with all his strength, and with all his mind, and he loved his neighbor as himself. So when the Law comes and accuses you of not having kept it, bid it go to Christ. Say, 'There is the Man who has kept it; to him I cling; he fulfilled it *for* me and gave his fulfillment *to* me.'"

Love in Action

I have seen that perfect love of Christ in action through God's people countless times. People like

Gil and Carmen Ramirez, Manny and Elisa Santiago, Carlos and Clara DelValle, and Ruth Barden, who selflessly care for foster children, radiating the same love they give their own kids. This is faith active in love. Like Ruth Wehmhoefer, elderly and infirm, but absolutely a warrior in prayer, hobbling about to visit the sick and bringing them her love of God's people. Simple acts of love in the home to those who are outcast and lonely and sick come from the righteous and loving heart of Christ within.

Love in Christ can lead as well to wrestling matches with the powers of this world. Just as the peace of God puts you in conflict with the forces of violence in the universe, so the love of God puts you in conflict with the forces of hostility in the universe. Love and peace in Christ can be fighting words.

Some of the most blighted and blasted inner city areas in the country are in my backyard. Chaos rules. Drive-by shootings and drug wars turn the streets into bullet bazaars. I have buried parishioners who were shot to death. Marie, an elderly woman, was raped, bound, gagged, and then set on fire. She was incinerated as her home burned down around her. She rests in peace in heaven, but her end on earth was hell. The perfect love of Christ must face down death and hell. It must be strong.

The week after Marie died, at a meeting in our church basement, The Lutheran Church—Missouri

Synod made the first million-dollar, interest-free loan commitment to begin a project called "The Nehemiah Plan." Fifty-five congregations representing a dozen different denominations have carried that plan forward.

The simple aim of the Nehemiah Plan is to rebuild inner-city neighborhoods from the ashes up by erecting and selling single-family homes at low cost. City fathers had to be convinced. Drug lords had to be evicted. Corruption had to be rooted out. The political systems that demand greasing had to be grease-proofed. Cooperation among Christians had to be real, and not just at the level of polite coffee table conversation. Black, Hispanic, and white parishioners had to grow in trust. Active love in Christ had to conquer all of this. And it did. He did.

The burned-out shell that was Marie's home has been torn down. A Nehemiah home stands in its place. Two thousand of those homes have created neighborhoods where destruction dominated.

I contend that only the perfect love of Christ, a love more powerful than death in the hearts of God's people across the narrow lines of church denominations, could bring the Nehemiah Plan to pass.

Gerald Holder, an elder in our church, who comes from Barbados, says, "I know that God's love is powerful. Jesus has saved me and my family. I have been baptized and have put on Christ. And that means everything to me. But the Nehemiah home where my family lives is a sign that God's love is strong enough to bring a neighborhood back from the ashes. I thank God for it."

Of course, Gerald is not content to sit home and rest. Faith acts in love. So Gerald Holder speaks from love to tell his friends and workmates about all that he has received. He has brought over 60 adults to church to join a community of Christian love.

If saving faith sits on its backside, how *faith*-full can it be? Saving faith from the outside in, from God's Word of grace to your heart, produces loving hearts that burn to tell the truth, to live out love. These flames do not bring death, but life.

The peace you have, the honesty you live, the love you explore, must be your own. These are very personal benefits of your perfection in Christ. But you are not left alone. There is one final benefit of our perfect righteousness in Christ. It involves you, and God, and all who trust in Christ. It is incredibly exciting news!

 **Chapter 18**

God Lives in Us: Life Perfected

I have been crucified with Christ and I no longer live, but Christ lives in me.
Galatians 2:20

"There is now no condemnation for those who are in Christ Jesus," thumps the gavel, echoing the hammering of your heartbeat. Through his Word, the Judge has declared you innocent. You are alive—in Christ!

In Christ

What does it mean to be "in Christ?" Jesus gave this promise to those who believe: "The Spirit of truth ... lives with you and will be in you. ... I am in my Father, and you are in me, and I am in you" (John 14:17, 20). Jesus is describing the dynamic movement of God.

What does saving faith produce? We know that

it works from the outside in, from the dot on the horizon where Christ covers that cinder with your name on it back into the person inhabiting the flesh and bones called you. We know it works. The dynamic of that working, bubbling, formative faith is that a dwelling place is hollowed out inside you for the Almighty God—Father, Son, and Holy Spirit. And there they abide, the Three-in-One and One-in-Three. God lives in *you!*

This is no spiritualized gimmick. I am not telling you that God lives in you the way your memories of sainted Aunt Alma live in you. I am not telling you that God lives in you whenever you think happy thoughts or whistle a happy tune. I am not telling you that God lives in you exclusively through the special "spiritual" gifts God gives you. I am talking about far, far more.

On the other hand, I am not telling you that you are now fully divine and may wave your pinky to receive proper homage from the kids and neighbors. Nor am I stating that we all carry that so-called mystical spark that flows like a river of lava into the unending energy stream of the great eternal ocean. You haven't tapped into some crazy New Age kind of electrical current here.

The fact that we are sinner-saints must never be forgotten. Each day I trust in Christ, who is for me, to cleanse my heart all over again. Honest, faithful confession and dependence on the merciful forgiveness of God remain at the center of my existence in Christ.

The Indwelling Christ

Profound, mysterious, wondrous promises of God are at work in you. Because Christ is *for* you, Christ comes *to* you and lives *in* you. On a daily basis, God stirs up that Christ in you. You are the habitation of the Most High God, the temple of the Holy Spirit. You can proclaim with Paul, "I no longer live, but Christ lives in me."

What does this mean? It means first of all that "to live is Christ" (Philippians 1:21). It means that in very real terms you have been where Christ has been and is now.

Read Romans 6:1–10. "Don't you know that all of us who were baptized into Christ Jesus were baptized into his death?" (v. 3). Then read also Galatians 2:15–21 and Ephesians 1:1–2:18.

Has Christ been crucified? Then you have been crucified.

Has Christ died? You have died.

Has Christ been buried? You have been buried.

Has Christ been raised? You have been raised.

Has Christ ascended? You have ascended.

By faith you are sitting at the banquet table in heaven's halls now, hidden with Christ in God. When the angel on Easter morning said, "He is not here; he has risen," you went along for the ride.

You have been where Christ has been and where Christ is. How would you express that? Read this incident from the life of our friend Martin Luther:

One day a stranger knocked on Luther's door. When the door opened, the stranger asked, "Does Martin Luther live here?"

"No," Luther answered. "He died. Christ lives here now."

Read Romans 6 again. By Baptism, you have been crucified, died, and have been buried with Christ. But do not lose hope!

Speaking about that angel's message on Easter morning, Luther said, "Christ is not here; hence a Christian must not be here. Your life is hid, not in a chest, for there it might be found, but in him who is nowhere. Our life is hidden high above our eyes, and high above all that we can feel." You have been raised to new life, ascended, and seated in "the heavenly realms" (Ephesians 2:6).

And yet there is more! It works both ways. Not only are you where Christ is, but Christ is where you are. This is where your perfect righteousness hits the streets running. This is what it means to live the perfect life. All that is Christ is in you. "In Christ all the fullness of the Deity lives in bodily form, and you have been given fullness in Christ," says Paul in Colossians 2:9. All that the Father is abides in you. All that the Comforter, the Holy Spirit, is dwells in you.

The Friend of Sinners is alive in you to befriend sinners. The Comforter is alive in you to comfort the wounded and broken-hearted. The Father is alive in you to run with love to the lost. The power of the living God to turn the world upside down is yours, for Christ lives in you. The power of love to confront the phony with the force of the Law so that true love in Christ might be revealed is yours. This is what it means to be a perfect saint of God. The righteousness of Christ accomplished outside you is brought to you.

I am absolutely convinced that this precious resource of faith has been overlooked in our time. We are so busy getting hopped up with every new wave of opinion, every well-organized program, every shortcut to an ultra-slim body and an ultra-fashionable church that we have ignored the most profound Christian reality: by grace through faith, on account of Christ, God lives in us!

Living in Christ

What in the world does this mean for your life? The horizons are limitless.

First there is eternal life. What I mean by "eternal life" is that when you face God you will find love—now, when you die, and after your body is buried. The famous horror-story author Stephen King, in one of his books, describes a tormented creature from beyond the grave. The creature cries the throwaway line, "Yes, there is life after death! I'm living it!" Let me turn that horror story on its ear. The you who is in Christ at the heavenly banquet table is able to cry out the same words, but in happy peace and joy, "Yes, there is life after death! I'm living it!"

Then, with eternal life there is love—again.

Because God lives in you, there is a real sense in which you are "in love" with God. By faith the most intimate relationship you possess is the relationship between you and God, with Christ in the middle.

Lord, you I love with all my heart.

You will I love, my strength, my tower;
You will I love, my hope, my joy;
You will I love with all my power,
With fervor time cannot destroy.

These lines are from two hymns written hundreds of years ago. They describe something precious, something valued above all else in the world. It is obvious that the authors were in love with God. There is no reason to be ashamed of stating it that way. I am not talking about dinner-date romance. I am talking about a love that is completely and totally intimate.

God not only knows me as I am and loves me in Christ, he is living in me through his Word of the Gospel. The living God has taken a room in *me*. This is a tenant, a roommate, I will never let go. This is a room I will set aside, clean and cherished. As Martin Luther prayed, "Ah, dearest Jesus, holy Child, make Thee a bed, soft, undefiled, within my heart, that it may be a quiet chamber kept for Thee." God has come to stay!

Paul talks about the reality of Christ's glory within by stating that we have this "treasure in jars of clay" (2 Corinthians 4:7). But there is really no adequate comparison. Does the President live in a homeless shelter? Is the Hope diamond on display at Wal-Mart? Does the Mona Lisa smile from a crate in your garage? No. Yet Christ lives in me, and my heart leaps to embrace him.

Life in Christ's Community

Then there is the community of believers. A church is not meant by God to be just a socially acceptable spot to spend a Sunday morning. That's American tradition at work. The community of believers is the assembly where Christ in you speaks to Christ in me and where the Word of God, which is "living and active ... sharper than any double-edged sword" (Hebrews 4:12), speaks to us both.

There is hunger in the Christian fellowship, a continuing hunger after righteousness and for the Righteous One, a hunger for faith to be fed by the Word. There is continuing hunger to give faith vibrant expression in worship and praise, in prayer, and in loving service. There is a deep-seated hunger to crack and bang at the barriers of evil and the Evil One with the explosive power of God at work. Why? Because the Lord is in his holy temple. *You* are one of those temples. The power of the community of God is the power to unify, magnify, and multiply the love of Christ within.

I know a church where the "passing of the peace" takes 20 minutes. The peace that transcends all understanding explodes in warmth and compassion and applause and hugs. Those under the press and strain of difficult times and bad decisions can find an authentic ministry of Christ—not just from the pastor, but from all of God's people in the Word and fellowship.

Everything that is Christ's is yours, including the true sharing of God's peace.

I know of a church where a girl named Keisha, age 10 at the time, came through the doors to receive a bag of food one day; assisted in the delivery of her own baby sister the next week at home; felt the presence of Christ in the church youth group in the following week; received instruction and stepped forward to be baptized with her sister six months later; and became, by age 11, a disciple bringing seven-, eight-, and nine-year-olds to Sunday school. The presence of the living Christ cannot be easily compartmentalized, case-loaded, or class and age designated. Jesus simply is where his people are. "I am with you always," he said (Matthew 28:20).

What is the most powerful single organization in the world? The Supreme Court? The Mafia? The United States Government? The world banking community? Sorry—you're not even close. The most powerful single organization in the world is the local community of believers—your Christian congregation. All the reality of righteousness is perfectly present to call to account and forgive, to strengthen and comfort, to battle and attack .

I cannot for the life of me figure out why people in so many churches seem listless and content to follow along limply, with eyes glazed over by early-morning doughnuts. We are engaged in a life-and-death struggle for souls of the lost. We are engaged daily in a life-and-death struggle with evil and the reality of human desperation before the Law of God. We are engaged because of the grace of God received through faith on account of Christ. We are engaged because God dwells within us in his Word of grace.

We are engaged. How can we be and act so *dis*engaged? Because of sin. And it must be faced honestly. All resources up to and including the indwelling presence of God have been given to us. Not to repent from the heart, not to listen hungrily to the Word, not to praise, not to share, not to thank, not to engage in common endeavor—what a tragedy! The devil laughs. But the devil will not have the last laugh! He cannot!

I know this much. God has loved me with an everlasting love in Christ Jesus. He lives within me. All that he is ... is mine. And yours. And ours.

In Christ we are God's "treasured possession" (Deuteronomy 7:6). We have a Priceless Treasure. We are perfectly right in Christ. Therefore, we can sing,

> Hence, all fears and sadness,
> For the Lord of gladness,
>   Jesus, enters in.
> Those who love the Father,

Though the storms may gather,
   Still have peace within.
For, whatever I must bear,
   Still in you lies purest pleasure,
   Jesus, priceless treasure!

DATE DUE			
APR 08 '96			
JUN 2 3 1999			